Exodus to Empowerment

Black Migration and the GOP

Angel Kaye

Table of Contents

Chapter 1

My journey: Navigating Community and Adversity

This is not a mere anecdote; it's my narrative. Born and raised in the bustling heart of New York City, I grew up embraced by the ideals and promises of the American government. In those formative years, I firmly believed that the government prioritized the welfare of Black Americans, especially as so many of us grappled with hardship. The pervasive reality of poverty among Black Americans shaped my understanding, leading me to trust that the Democratic Party was sincerely invested in uplifting those in need. This conviction sprang from the lived experiences of my community, which at one time appeared to flourish.

In my youth, I witnessed a vibrant Black community thriving in my neighborhood. Medical clinics provide essential healthcare services, connecting us with doctors and specialists. Supermarkets and pharmacies were accessible, ensuring we lacked for nothing. Our neighborhoods radiated vitality, fostering a childhood belief that someone truly cared for our well-being. In my eyes, we were affluent; our community's strength translated into a sense of prosperity.

Gradually, however, change crept in. At around ten years old, I observed a wave of newcomers from various ethnic backgrounds settling into our community. They spoke unfamiliar languages and often seemed to come from predominantly white backgrounds. Puerto Ricans and Dominicans began to populate our streets, signaling a shift in our community's dynamics. Though I didn't fully comprehend the implications then, I sensed a profound transformation underway. Eventually, I moved to North Carolina to live with my mother's family, where I navigated the complexities of adolescence into early adulthood.

After completing high school, I returned to New York City, eager to reunite with my mother and siblings. What I encountered upon my return left me in shock. The once-vibrant Black community I treasured had become unrecognizable. The clinics, pharmacies, and supermarkets critical to our neighborhoods had vanished. Now, our communities were a diverse blend of Black Americans and Hispanics. The illness and despair I encountered within the community were heart-wrenching. I was filled with questions: Why was this happening? Who was accountable? Although I understood that New York was governed by a democratic system, I struggled to fathom how such neglect could manifest.

As I grappled with my uncertain future and contemplated pursuing higher education or a trade, I resolved to follow an educational path that enabled me to assist others. I enrolled in the NYU School of Dentistry to study Dental Assisting. Despite the program's rigorous demands, I committed myself wholeheartedly, earning an Advanced Certificate in the field. As graduation approached, our class participated in mock job interviews, during which we were encouraged to target salaries of at least $14.00 per hour—the minimum wage at that time was a mere $4.25.

Excitement welled up within me as I recognized that this certificate equipped me to earn significantly above the minimum wage. Yet, my multiple job interviews often resulted in disappointing outcomes. Many employers offered me only $6.00 an hour, far below my expectations. Confusion and heartbreak enveloped me when two fellow Black students shared identical lowball offers with me and our white classmates received their desired salary.

At just nineteen, I faced the stark realities of racism directly. Here we stood, three diligent young Black individuals, yet we were presented with negligible salaries. The experience stung deeply, particularly because I had earned a place on the A honor roll. With no viable alternatives, we begrudgingly accepted these positions, convincing ourselves that the experience would lead to better pay in the future.

Over the following years, I gained valuable experience in the Dental Assistant field, yet I was confronted with an unexpected barrier—bilingualism became a prerequisite for job applicants. What had once been an accessible profession now seemed to favor immigrant Latino candidates, leaving Black Americans marginalized. An invisible barrier had been erected, isolating me from opportunities that had previously been within reach.

I witnessed this transformation unfold before my eyes. Hispanic individuals ascended into positions of authority, occupying roles that had once belonged to Black Americans. Again, I questioned who was directing these changes and whether our elected representatives truly advocated for our community. I observed that as new waves of Black immigrants from the Caribbean and Africa entered the country, they received resources and support that eluded those of us who had long been here. The government provided them with benefits that seemed unattainable for those who had fought for their place for generations.

In my frustration and disappointment, I turned inward. I focused on my family, deepening my spiritual relationship with God. Becoming a stay-at-home mother meant relying on entitlement programs for support. I enrolled my children in public schools, hoping they would receive the quality education I had experienced in the South. However, I was met with a disheartening reality.

The public schools in New York City were in dire condition. The buildings stood as relics of neglect, with unsanitary bathrooms and insufficient facilities. I was struck by the stark contrast between what I had envisioned and the disarray I encountered in a state governed by democratically elected officials tasked with serving the community's needs. This was my awakening. In my despair, I turned to prayer, seeking divine guidance for the path forward for my family.

Educating my children became my focal point amidst this grim reality. Though I didn't fully homeschool them, I took control of their learning journey. I aspired for them to grasp the importance of knowledge, faith, and resilience. During this period, I also enrolled in classes at a local college, driven by a desire to become an agent of change. I felt compelled to advocate for our children and the quality of education they rightfully deserved.

As time passed, I noticed significant shifts among the staff of the entitlement programs I relied upon. The predominantly white employees were replaced by immigrants from Jamaica, Barbados, and other Black nations. These new staff members often added complications rather than solutions, dealing with clients in an outright discourteous and dismissive manner.

The broader labor market dynamics reflected a systemic shift, leaving me bewildered by the reality. It felt as if we were being systematically excluded from opportunities we had long battled for. Eventually, when my children required less of my presence, I resolved to further my education rather than taking a couple of classes, I decided to take a semester and attend college full-time.

Choosing to study political science stemmed from my commitment to fostering change within my community, driven by a desire to learn and understand why the Black community consistently supported the Democratic Party. What was the basis of this unwavering allegiance? Did the Democratic Party genuinely deserve the loyalty that the Black community afforded it, and was this loyalty reciprocated? I felt compelled to research to uncover the role that the Democratic Party played in the advancement of Black Americans since its inception.

I earned my Bachelor's degree in Political Science, complemented by a minor in Health Education and Promotion. My education on the Democratic Party during my studies was quite superficial. I sensed a significant omission regarding the Party's role in fostering upward mobility for Black Americans from the era of slavery to the present day.

This ambiguity not only left me puzzled but also ignited my curiosity about what was being concealed. It became abundantly clear that the Democratic Party's primary focus is on immigrants. Interestingly, the Party appears to be attempting to replace Black Americans with Black foreign immigrants, an endeavor that is fundamentally flawed for numerous reasons: they do not speak for us, nor do they understand or care about the struggles faced by Black Americans in this country, which means there is no authentic connection to our experiences.

Ultimately, you cannot replace an entire nation of people. The idea that Black foreign-born individuals should have a voice in determining what is best for Black Americans is simply absurd. Furthermore, I recognized the intentional division sown between low- to middle-class Black and White Americans, driven by the Democratic Party's strategy of introducing divisive issues to keep us at odds. Why?

My personal goal was to secure a job that could accommodate my children's schedules. I am grateful for the part-time position I eventually obtained, as it allowed me to be present for my children while striving for a better future for all of us.

Yet, the environment at my new workplace took me by surprise. I quickly became aware that the majority of my colleagues were immigrants. While I held no personal grievances against them, I could not overlook how Black Americans were significantly underrepresented in our office. Unfortunately, I witnessed firsthand how Black immigrants refuse to understand the Challenges of Black Americans in America

The presence of Black immigrants in low-income Black American communities presents a complex situation. These immigrants come from various countries, each with its unique history and culture. When they settle in predominantly Black American neighborhoods, their different backgrounds and experiences affect local dynamics in unexpected ways. It created tensions and misunderstandings between the long-time residents and the newcomers.

These immigrants often brought their ideas about community, culture, and social issues, which did not align with the established views of residents. For instance, they prioritize different economic strategies and community organizing techniques. This led to friction, as each group had contrasting beliefs about what actions were most beneficial. Another prime example stems from my personal experience.

As a breastfeeding consultant, the program director told me that Black American women simply didn't want to breastfeed and that it would be a waste of time and resources to educate them. She said that in her country, Black women already understand the importance of breastfeeding, so they do it. At that moment, I realized that, as a Black immigrant leading a program aimed at helping Black American women and their babies, this woman didn't comprehend their struggles and didn't care to learn. She didn't recognize that understanding culture is crucial in making choices about breastfeeding.

Each community has its narratives and motivations for either supporting or opposing breastfeeding. Many Black American women may have profound historical reasons that shape their perspectives on breastfeeding. Issues such as distrust of the medical system due to past injustices, social pressures, and negative perceptions regarding breastfeeding in public all contribute significantly. These factors can complicate decision-making, and suggestions that seem beneficial might overlook the specific needs of the community.

I struggled to understand why a well-qualified Black American was overlooked for the position of directing a program aimed at serving Black American prenatal and postpartum women, while instead, a Black immigrant was appointed who lacks concern for the community she serves. Being of one race does not equate to shared experiences; Black people come from diverse walks of life, and it is our cultural and tribal affiliations that create distinctions. The absence of empathy and self-awareness regarding this diversity is what fuels conflicts. It was disheartening to discover that this trend spanned beyond my workplace, permeating the entire metro area of New York City.

Due to these differences, the work that some immigrants are brought in to do can inadvertently contribute to existing problems rather than solve them. There might be instances where immigrants are hired to engage with the community, but because they don't fully grasp the local issues, their efforts can end up opposing what the community needs. This scenario results in a dilemma that may exacerbate issues rather than provide solutions, causing frustration for long-time residents who feel their voices are not being heard.

Working within these communities often requires deep understanding and empathy toward the historical and ongoing struggles faced by Black Americans. Without that insight, well-meaning efforts can misfire. An example of this can be seen in community development projects that do not consider the unique needs and priorities of residents. If these projects are designed without input from the community, they may not only fail but could also perpetuate existing injustices.

Another aspect to consider is the unique struggles of Black Americans compared to those of Black immigrants. Many immigrants come with a perspective shaped by their experiences in their countries of origin. For instance, they may have faced challenges regarding economic opportunities or discrimination based on their national backgrounds. However, they might not have firsthand knowledge of the specific historical context and systemic barriers that Black Americans encounter in the United States. This disconnect can lead to confusion and a lack of support for those in desperate need of help.

Black Americans actively sought collaboration with Black immigrants; however, what they faced was an overwhelming tide of hatred and systemic cultural discrimination that deepened existing divides. Black Americans recognized the crucial importance of fostering environments where everyone feels comfortable sharing their experiences and perspectives. They understood that engaging in this dialogue could potentially lead to a deeper understanding of each other's circumstances, and acknowledged how vital this was for developing a unified approach to addressing community challenges. They had simply been waiting for the exchange.

What remains largely unrecognized is the crucial role of educational resources within Black American spaces. The socioeconomic disparities that Black Americans encounter in their respective environments are alarming and require urgent attention. There exists a profound necessity for organizations to take proactive steps in facilitating workshops and training sessions aimed at educating millennials, their descendants, and long-term residents. These initiatives are essential to empower individuals to join the workforce, thereby enabling them to achieve upward mobility. It is imperative to foster a culture of understanding, prioritizing collaboration and support over persistent resistance, to create pathways for a brighter, more equitable future for Black Americans first.

Unfortunately, this reflects the deep-rooted oppression that Black Americans face as immigration flows into our borders with the potential to marginalize an entire nation of people. The challenge began in the early

1980s with the influx of Latino and Black foreign-born immigrants, and today, Democrats are exacerbating this situation with the twenty-one million who have recently arrived on our shores.

I struggle to perceive this as a mere coincidence. The harrowing reality that Black Americans confront amid this wave of immigrant replacement also applies to white working-class Americans earning seventy thousand dollars and below. White Americans are being targeted with immigrant replacement as well. The spot-light of the challenges they are facing may be slightly grim due in part to the primary distinction which lies in demographics; Black Americans constitute a smaller percentage of the population in the U.S. compared to whites, making it more apparent to recognize the glaring disparities.

Leaders often time neglect the individuals they are supposed to serve. Policymakers and political organizers carry a significant responsibility to ensure their choices prioritize the needs of Americans above all else. By actively involving Black Americans in the policymaking process, they can ensure that the solutions implemented genuinely meet the needs of the Black American community. This inclusion would involve guaranteeing that every American has access to a well-paying, unionized job with retirement benefits before welcoming immigrants into an already strained economy. Feedback on proposed initiatives is essential, along with a demonstrated willingness to prioritize Americans first.

Chapter 2

Government Compassion for Americans

Compassion is an essential quality that any government should have. When government officials demonstrate genuine care for their citizens, it establishes a standard for how society should operate. It signals to everyone that the well-being of individuals is valued. This can include actions like providing necessary support services, improving public health, and ensuring security for all. For example, when governments invest in healthcare, they show that they care about the health and well-being of their citizens. This not only leads to a healthier population but also fosters a sense of community. People feel supported when they know their needs are being prioritized.

It's important to build Trust and Support

When the American government puts its citizens first, it helps build a community founded on trust and mutual support. This trust encourages citizens to engage more with their government and other Americans. Consider examples of trust-building initiatives, such as community forums where citizens can voice concerns and express their needs. These initiatives allow the government to better understand the issues their citizens face. As people see their concerns being addressed, they feel more connected and invested in their community. In contrast, when compassion is absent, it leads to feelings of neglect and isolation, undermining the very fabric of society.

The Consequences of Lack of Compassion

When the American government lacks compassion and does not prioritize the needs of its own citizens, it creates conflict and division. This often happens when citizens feel as if they are in direct competition with immigrants. Instead of uniting, people may scapegoat each other for jobs, housing, and other resources. It is critical to understand that this competition is fueled by systemic issues rather than individual choices. For instance, if a local job scarcity leads to tensions between immigrants and native citizens, the root cause is not the immigrants but rather the lack of job opportunities and economic development due to the American government's refusal to put the needs of its citizens first.

Prioritizing Citizens' Needs

Americans should not have to compete with immigrants for jobs or wages. Job competition can lead to resentment and divisions that further stir conflict. The American government needs to address these concerns by prioritizing the needs of its citizens first. This could mean implementing job training programs, expanding educational opportunities, or creating new job positions. For example, government-funded vocational training can help prepare citizens for available jobs. By ensuring that citizens are well-prepared for the workforce, the government shows commitment to their growth and success.

Fair Hiring Practices

The Democratic Party should be a party for all American citizens and should take proactive steps to create a fair job market. This includes implementing policies that prevent employers from choosing to hire immigrant workers over citizens just to save on wages. It should be illegal for companies to disregard American workers in favor of immigrant labor unless there is a significant reason for doing so, such as poor job performance. Ensuring such laws are in place can protect job security for American workers. This should be complemented by incentives for companies that employ citizens, which encourages more businesses to invest in the local workforce. That's called putting Americans first.

Creating a Clear Path for Collaboration

In welcoming immigrants, the American government should not only focus on the needs of newcomers but also craft a clear path that benefits all parties. It could establish mentorship programs that connect immigrants with American workers, promoting collaboration rather than competition. This facilitation can lead to a sharing of skills and experiences, enhancing workplace environments. For example, a company may have a diverse team where both immigrants and American workers learn from each other's backgrounds and insights. Which can bring forth positive collaboration. Instead of creating a workplace environment where immigrant workers outnumber Americans in the workforce. This type of inequality creates conflict and division.

Understanding the balance between supporting citizens and welcoming immigrants is crucial. Equal opportunities must be provided not just to immigrants but also to American workers to avoid any feelings of dispossession. Programs that help citizens gain skills necessary for industries that are growing should be an integral part of the American government's strategy for its citizens. Furthermore, creating policies that encourage businesses to focus on local talent can help maintain job certainty for American citizens while still allowing immigrants to contribute economically.

Building a Unified Community

Ultimately, the goal is to create a more unified community where all individuals feel valued, regardless of their background. The government plays a critical role in shaping this community through compassion and fair practices. Activating community service initiatives that serve both citizens and immigrants can further reinforce the notion that everyone matters. For example, programs that encourage volunteering can help bridge gaps in understanding and connection. When citizens and immigrants work together, they can develop relationships based on trust, leading to a more cohesive society.

White and Black Americans deserve openness and transparency in communication from our government. For far too long, our government has courted our votes while largely ignoring our needs. As citizens of the United States, we have often felt marginalized and overlooked. Our government has neglected us, failing to address the pressing issues that affect our lives. The Democrats have held office for most of the past twelve years, crafting American policies that primarily benefit immigrants, which has left Black and White citizens embroiled in divisive debates over issues like abortion rights.

This division only deepens the rift among us. Systematically, Black and White poor Americans have been disenfranchised from the voting process, as the Democratic Party has lacked meaningful laws or policies that truly support our communities. It often feels as though immigrants have become the focus, while Black and poor White Americans are treated as second-class citizens. This favoritism toward immigrants exacerbates the divide among different demographics. The refusal of the government to unite immigrants and longtime residents points to an upcoming election landscape that appears increasingly polarized, pitting immigrants against Americans.

Society pretends ignorance toward the profound anger that many Americans feel regarding the nation's persistent immigration policies. The American government ought to prioritize the well-being of its own citizens. If American citizens enjoyed job security, access to comprehensive training, free education, and the ability to purchase homes, we wouldn't witness such a stark divide or conflict with immigrants arriving in America.

Unfortunately, that is not our reality. Immigrants from diverse backgrounds—Black, European, and Asian—are flocking to America, drawn by various monetary incentives, and they are competing fiercely with economically disadvantaged Black and White middle-class Americans in the job market, often emerging victorious. This perceived inequality is deeply unjust. I cannot think of any country that offers better treatment to its immigrants than it does to its own citizens. This situation is at the heart of the growing divide and the increasing animosity we see towards different demographics by both ends of the political spectrum.

The question I find myself grappling with—and I direct this, particularly at the Democratic Party, which has held power for over a decade—is: why would Democrats foster a climate of resentment between immigrants and American citizens? Immigrants are not the root of the problem. It is, rather, the Democrats' policies that seem focused on benefiting immigrants while neglecting the needs of citizens. Corporations enthusiastically support these immigration policies, as evidenced by their hiring practices. For decades now, they have favored immigrant workers over Black and White Americans, and this trend is becoming increasingly conspicuous. We are witnessing companies outright firing American workers in favor of immigrants.

Some American companies have even begun to outsource to foreign firms, which in turn replace American employees with foreign workers. This pattern appears to be intentional as if everyone is complicit. Lawyers often refrain from intervening, and the government has turned a blind eye to the unequal employment opportunities it has purposefully created.

As a result, the economic prospects for both Black and White middle-class Americans continue to decline while the immigrant economy flourishes.

What I have come to understand is that America isn't just a country; it's a corporation. America operates as a legal entity with numerous responsibilities and generates substantial profit. It has 100 shareholders who are the owners of this corporation, providing financial backing through lobbyists in exchange for economic gains throughout the life of the corporation—America itself.

These shareholders are the decision-makers, pulling the strings and directing the agenda. America conducts business globally; in exchange for the business ventures that American corporations pursue, they allow citizens from these foreign countries to come to America and open businesses. As an incentive, these foreigners bring along their fellow citizens to America and place them in positions of power, where they are allowed to thrive. There have been many instances where foreigners buy businesses, fire American workers, and hire their foreign-born countrymen. America claims they have the legal right to do so. This is why we are now seeing an enormous number of foreign businesses in America.

Most foreigners who come to America do not necessarily start at the bottom; rather, they often enter the American job market with an advantage, earning six-figure salaries. The only poor immigrants arriving in America are typically those from Black and Brown countries, placed in

Black and White middle-class spaces to create conflict and distraction. It is a camouflage used to misdirect attention from the fact that the American corporation is now predominantly run by foreigners from other countries with whom the American corporation does business.

For this corporation to remain profitable, it requires a vast workforce. Initially, the American Corporation relied on immigrant labor for its economic advantages. However, it has become evident that Black and White middle Americans—its core contributors—have grown weary of being exploited, disillusioned by empty promises, and frustrated by witnessing their nation decline due to ineffective policies.

Black and White middle-class Americans represent the original union members of this nation, yet we have been systematically disenfranchised. America Corp. has long worked to divide its citizens, pitting them against one another through unjust policies and inadequate wages. However, a growing awareness is emerging among Black and White middle-class: the division was a manipulated narrative crafted by our government to sustain internal conflict. We are beginning to recognize that our shared experiences and commonalities far outweigh our differences.

This newfound understanding poses a significant challenge for the government, which seeks to conjure yet another divide—one that creates a new group of workers who will not only perpetuate division but also align with the government's prioritized issues. In return, they are promised the best jobs America has to offer along with enticing financial incentives. The only way America Corp. can achieve this is by replacing its own citizens, fostering a new divide between Americans and immigrants.

Chapter 3

The Problem is Not The Immigrants, It's The Immigration Policy

This is why I will reiterate, as many times as necessary, that American citizens have no issues with immigrants. The true concern lies within the Democratic Party's immigration policies, which are designed to replace American workers and provide incentives and jobs to new workers—the immigrants. Naturally, this will create a divide, exactly as the Democrats intend. This country cannot function without conflict and division. Middle-class Black and White people must unite and demonstrate that we have more in common than what separates us. Open and honest dialogue is essential, and we must realize that everyone deserves fair treatment. America is a Corporation and its shareholders have committed a grave disservice to union members—Black and White citizens alike—and we deserve to be treated justly.

The American Corporation is trying to portray that Black and White middle-class Americans harbor resentment towards immigrants, which is not the case. I don't know of any citizen who is content witnessing harsh treatment from their government while seeing foreigners being granted preferential treatment. Black and White middle-class Americans have issues with the American government. This is less about immigrants and more about corporate government policy. American is a Corporation that is well aware of the uncompromising position it has put its union members in. Rather than address our concerns, they are looking to not only create a distraction but also foster conflict and division among its citizens and the immigrants. This is class warfare.

The disparity between social classes in America, as it acts as a Corporation, highlights a troubling reality. The Black and White middle class is caught in a tug-of-war. The White middle class, once holding significant power, now feels the pressure of economic decline as jobs are shifted overseas or handed to foreigners. Meanwhile, the Black middle class, often seen as a token presence in this landscape, faces systemic barriers that further entrench their socioeconomic struggles. This dynamic creates a complicated situation where both groups compete for limited resources and opportunities, fueling resentment rather than understanding.

Many feel displaced, and unable to find stable employment. Small businesses close down as foreign entities take over. It's not just the loss of jobs; it's a loss of identity, security, and community. Families struggle to make ends meet, and children bear the brunt of this economic instability. The narrative pushed by the media often overlooks these realities. Instead of shedding light on the struggles faced by the middle class, the focus remains on the successes of a few, creating an illusion of prosperity while neglecting the vast majority who don't share in that wealth.

As the American Corporation evolves, it embarks on a path that favors profit over people. The voices of the underprivileged are drowned out in boardrooms where decisions are made far removed from the lives affected by these corporate moves. Politicians promise change, yet little is done to address the core issues that create and sustain this socioeconomic disparity. The cycle perpetuates itself, with education becoming a privilege rather than a right. Those who can afford it navigate a path to success, while others are left behind. Those who manage to obtain a degree are being passed over to foreign degree holders instead.

Within this structure arises a false sense of community. The middle class, attempting to uphold their position, often turns against one another, pointing fingers at the foreign workforce instead of recognizing the system that benefits from this division. The dialogue shifts from seeking unity to blame games, further fracturing the fragile bonds that once held communities together. Neighbors turn against neighbors, and the focus shifts away from the real issues at hand, allowing American corporations to continue their operations unchallenged. The real dilemma lies not in who is taking the jobs but in why the system is failing to provide equitable opportunities for all.

The Black and white middle-class communities in America have come to realize the purpose of this divide. This is also the reason for the shift in party lines among Black American men. Black American males see the enmity the Democratic Party has created between them and Black American women, particularly regarding attempts to structurally rebuild two-parent family households within the Black community. This is yet another reason Black American males are abandoning the Democratic Party.

Black and white middle-class workers recognize the Democratic strategy to divide them through unfair immigration policies, inadequate wealth distribution, and the implementation of policies that encourage us to judge and demonize one another.

Amidst this chaos, grassroots movements have emerged. Black and white middle-class Americans have united to reclaim their voices, demanding access to jobs, fair wages, and equitable treatment. We share stories of struggle, illustrating the harsh realities of living in a society that prioritizes profit over people. These movements will grow because they are fueled by a collective desire for change; we must push back against the corporate agenda that seems to dictate every aspect of our lives.

The fight transcends mere economics; it revolves around America as a corporation prioritizing loyalty to its citizens. It involves recognizing and valuing both Black and White American middle-class workers and ensuring that we are not relegated to second-class status. It is imperative to allocate resources that foster security and stability for our families. This struggle is for Black and White American children and future generations to have access to opportunities in America and a rightful place at the table that we have helped create. It's about dignity. It's about respect. It's about our fundamental right to earn a living wage worthy of our contributions, especially at a time when our nation seems to be transforming into something unrecognizable.

Chapter 4

Black And White Americans

Unity

This struggle transcended color lines, uniting Black and White middle-class Americans in pursuit of a shared goal. We possess far more in common than what divides us, yet the American Government has exploited that unity, leveraging the issues we disagree on to polarize us. Instead of simply agreeing to disagree, we've allowed our government to weaponize our differences, transforming them into divisions that prevent us from finding common ground. Our government has systematically institutionalized these disagreements, embedding them into policy rather than fostering understanding and cooperation.

Instead of the Black and white Middle-class agreeing to disagree on the issue of whether you see the moralistic implications behind it, we should have been able to acknowledge one another by saying, "That's your reasoning, that's the position you have taken, and I will not judge you." I will not judge you because I'm not God; that's between you and God, so let's move on.

However, we didn't make that distinction, and because of this, we have allowed the American government to use this as a tool that will forever keep us divided. We have permitted our government to weave it into the fabric of our daily lives, keeping us playing God and judging one another perpetually. Some decisions that women make should be viewed as a private reality between them and God, and we shouldn't refrain from passing judgment or allow our government to be involved. If our government wants to get involved, it can be done by way of finding a solution to the issue. Don't just say the building is on fire and point to who is to blame for the fire without providing water to put the fire out.

Many preventative measures could eliminate judgmental issues without rendering them lawful and divisive. We could start a foundation that provides low-income women with genuine education and career opportunities, healthcare, housing, services, and other basic support they need to fulfill their obligations. This funding wouldn't come from taxpayers; instead, it would come from philanthropists and celebrities alike, similar to the March of Dimes.

The March of Dimes is a foundation that generates over a billion dollars a year in revenue, along with many other foundations in America. Some might argue that, in these foundations, excluding St. Jude's, the donations never reach the intended target, which is unfortunate. With the right leadership and commitment, we can ensure that all women have access to quality education, the ability to gain information, and the necessary means to prevent unfortunate circumstances from arising.

We should strive to be a nation that wholeheartedly supports families, establishing resources that empower family structures to thrive instead of demonizing and turning a sensitive issue into a divisive political battleground.

Low- and middle-class Black and White Americans need to realize that we are stronger together than we are apart. We have more in common than what separates us. We must speak with those among our tribes who refuse to form alliances and educate them on doing what's best for the greater good of our country and the well-being of our generations to come. Once we form alliances we will gain momentum.

It is then that the voices of the Black and White middle-class marginalized Americans will gain traction as more people join our cause. We need to organize rallies and awareness campaigns, calling on leaders to recognize the true fabric of America: support, resilience, and the potential for change. The narrative will start to shift. People will begin to understand that the battle needs to be fought together, regardless of race or background. Allies form unexpectedly, standing shoulder to shoulder, united by a shared understanding of our plight. This collective action serves to highlight the disparities between those who benefit from the system and those who do not. Together we will gain momentum and leverage.

As these movements gain momentum, corporate America takes notice. Change doesn't happen overnight; it is a gradual process that requires persistent effort and unwavering commitment. Each step forward will be met with resistance, as the entrenched interests of the powerful fight to maintain the status quo. Challenges are abundant, yet there is a palpable sense of hope that runs through the ranks of all of us advocating for change. As the discussions grow more pointed, we will begin to shine a light on the systemic injustices that have long been ignored.

We will form a new alliance with the understanding that true progress comes when everyone has a stake. America The Corporation will begin to recognize that the issues are not simply about competition for jobs but about building a sustainable future. They push back against the narrative of scarcity creating opportunities that benefit all Americans. The conversations become richer when both Black and White middle-class voices are in alignment, allowing for more innovative solutions to arise. It's about building an equitable society for low and middle-class Black and White Americans first.

The pursuit of profit at the expense of people affects Blacks and Whites in middle America who have been in this country since its inception. Black and White low and middle-class Americans need allies. Coincidently enough Black Americans only hear from our Black celebrities every four years during the presidential election. Black Americans need to know that our Black Celebrities understand that no changes have been made to improve the socio-economic issues that Blacks are going through in this country. We need Black celebrities to connect more with their Black counterparts who are actively engaged in the community.

Chapter 5

Black American Celebrities

Overseers

Black American celebrities must forge genuine partnerships within the Black communities. Once you achieve celebrity status, your connection to the struggles of Black communities diminishes; you no longer directly witness the socioeconomic challenges that your fellow Black citizens confront daily. When members of the Black middle class illuminate issues in low-income neighborhoods, take their insights seriously. Support their willingness to transcend party lines.

Your financial stability means the decisions of America The Corporation may not impact you directly, so it is essential to heed the voices of those affected and leverage your influence to advocate for the changes we seek. We would greatly appreciate your support. However, if you fail to invest in these underserved communities by directing resources toward education, arts, or after-school programs, then simply showing up every four years to instruct Black individuals on their voting choices is comparable to returning to a plantation to decide which master to serve for another term of oppression.

America operates like an immense corporation, and all of us, including the Black celebrities, are just pieces on the chessboard. The only distinction lies in your financial resources, which grant you influence. This influence should be harnessed to uplift your communities. At the very least, we ask you to become our allies. We have supported your careers by purchasing your music, attending your concerts, and watching your films. All we seek is reciprocity in this political arena. Some of you may face challenges as you rise to the top and subsequently use your influence to manipulate electoral outcomes, which is disheartening. My mother used to say, "Kaye, if you can't help them, fine, but don't hurt them.

"

If, for any reason, Black celebrities choose not to utilize your resources to allocate funding in our neighborhoods, that's understandable. However, please do not further harm us. Simply be our allies. Should you opt not to engage, then keep your voting preferences private. If you cannot aid someone, that's acceptable, but refrain from causing them harm! Amidst the shocking revelations emerging throughout the music, film, and entertainment industry, Black Americans are increasingly perceiving Black celebrity influencers as lacking genuine influence. However, we still seek your support. It's essential to recognize that reciprocity involves a mutual exchange, and so far, the Black community has yet to experience that fair give-and-take from our Black celebrity counterparts.

I feel a song coming on:

Woo, ooh
Woo, ooh

I was the third brother of five

Doing whatever I had to do to survive

I'm not saying what I did was alright

Tryna break out of the ghetto was a day-to-day fight

been down so long, getting up didn't cross my mind

But I knew there was a better way of life, and I was just trying to find

You don't know what you'll do until you're put under pressure

'Cross 110th Street is a hell of a tester

Across 110th Street

Pimps trying to catch a woman that's weak

Across 110th Street

Pushers won't let the junkie go free

Across 110th Street

Woman trying to catch a trick on the street, ooh baby

Across 110th Street

You can find it all in the street

Woo, ooh, oh

I got one more thing I'd like to talk to y'all about right now

Hey brother, there's a better way out

Snorting that coke, shooting that dope, man, you're copping out

Take my advice, it's either live or die

You've got to be strong if you wanna survive

The family on the other side of town

Would catch hell without a ghetto around

In every city you'll find the same thing going down

Harlem is the capital of every ghetto town

Help me sing it

Across 110th Street

Pimps trying to catch a woman that's weak

Across 110th Street

Pushers won't let the junkie go free, oh

Across 110th Street

A woman trying to catch a trick on the street, ooh baby

Across 110th Street, look

You can find it all in the street...

Yes, you can

Oh, look around you, look around you, look around you

Look around you, uh, yeah

Woo, ooh

Chapter 6

The History of Voting In Black America

Voting is the primary occasion when the voice of Americans appears to carry weight. As a Black American voter, when the Presidential election approaches, I resonate with the sentiment expressed in Womack's song about "pimps trying to catch a woman that's weak." My goal transcends merely casting my vote; I aspire to comprehend the political landscape in its entirety. I strive to listen to both candidates, free from the influence of left or right-wing ideology, bias, and propaganda. It is my responsibility to remain informed and conduct thorough research, enabling me to make a well-considered decision about who will best serve my family, community, and country. I neither seek nor welcome outside interference in my decision-making process.

I recognize the necessity of being well-versed in political issues to grasp what is at stake, determine whom to support, and identify those who genuinely prioritize my interests. As a voter, it is vital for me to understand not only the historical context of voting and its impact on shaping our communities and society but also how I have personally benefited from this system. My research has led me to the realization that the Democratic Party has not been kind or fair to Black Americans, both before and after the era of slavery. This evidence prompts me to reflect, but more importantly, I find myself questioning why Black Americans maintain such unwavering loyalty to a party that hasn't demonstrated a commitment to resolving the issue they've faced for generations.

The Division of Voting in America

Voting in America plays a crucial role in shaping the political landscape, with its impact evident in the division of our nation into two distinct factions. Each side believes in the superiority of its ideals, creating a significant barrier for there to be no cooperation. This division is not merely an abstract concept; it manifests in the operational dynamics and interactions of political parties. When voters align themselves with a particular party, they often adopt a mindset that prioritizes loyalty to that party over the possibility of collaboration with others. This type of political collaboration seeps into the media as well. The reluctance to work together has profound implications for government functionality and the policies that are enacted. Black and white middle-class Americans have had their issues fragmented between two factions, and our voices have not been heard. When we come together to fight for the same cause, they have no choice but to listen.

The Consequences of Partisan Strategies

Instead of seeking common ground, political factions are more likely to engage in partisan strategies. These strategies are designed to benefit the parties in power rather than the general public. For instance, politicians craft laws that appeal to their base while ignoring the needs and concerns of the opposition. This method of governance has led to a cycle of mistrust and animosity, making it even harder to unify the country. As average citizens, this partisanship has become frustrating. Americans are feeling that their representatives are not addressing the issues they care about because they are too focused on winning political battles rather than improving the country.

Historical Context of Political Parties

To understand the current state of political division in America, it is crucial to look back at the history of the major political parties. The Democratic Party, for instance, has a complicated and often contradicted American history. At one time, it was the democratic party that supported slavery, with leaders who frequently opposed Civil Rights laws. This historical context is essential for grasping how political affiliations can shape opinions and influence actions over time. For example, when we delve into the past, we see that it was the Radical Republican Party that championed the end of slavery. They fought vigorously for the emancipation of enslaved individuals and worked tirelessly to establish Civil Rights for Black Americans. It was the Republicans and Abraham Lincoln who resolutely called for the abolition of slavery, marking a significant turning point in American history.

The Role of Extremism

During certain periods in history, particularly during the Reconstruction era, it was the democratic party in alliance with extremist groups such as the Ku Klux Klan. The Klan emerged as a force to stop the progress being made by Black Americans under the advisement of the democratic party. Understanding this relationship is crucial because it highlights how the democratic party has historically sought to maintain power over Black Americans through fear and intimidation. This kind of extremism contributed to deeper societal divisions and has left lasting scars on the fabric of American society. Today, it is essential to recognize the long-lasting effects of such alliances and the role they play in ongoing political debates.

The Need for Understanding and Collaboration

As we, the voters, navigate the current political landscape, it is important to emphasize the need for understanding and collaboration. We must recognize that, despite differences in ideology, working together is vital for progress. This entails actively seeking opportunities for dialogue with those who hold differing views. It also involves ensuring that the media understands that we are the people they need to interview and engage with regarding issues that matter most in our communities. Much to often we see the media interviewing the elite discussing issues that matter to us most that they don't understand. We must hold the media responsible for misinforming the population because of their own biases to further push their agenda.

During election seasons, the media has taken a biased approach, tending to speak with the factions they support the most. American citizens used to count on the media to remain neutral, tell the truth, examine both sides and engage with citizens from Black and White communities.

Furthermore, the media would allow Americans to make their own decisions instead of making them for us. Unfortunately, it seems the current agenda for the media is to shape the opinions of American citizens through propaganda embellishments, ad hominem attacks on the opposition, and meaningless rhetoric.

Building a More Cooperative Political Culture

If we aspire to cultivate a more cooperative political culture, it is essential to engage in respectful dialogue. Name-calling constitutes a form of bullying. We observe the media fostering mudslinging when their candidates are trailing, and children witness adults behaving immaturely. Such behavior is inexcusable. I do not claim to be righteous in this matter; I have had to check myself several times. However, both sides must commit to listening and comprehending rather than aggressively defending their positions. We can organize community events aimed at collaboration, whether through volunteer work or local advocacy projects. When we unite to tackle community issues, we illustrate our ability to transcend our differences to achieve a shared goal.

Historical Lessons for Modern Politics

In addition to fostering collaboration and understanding, reflecting on historical lessons can provide valuable insights into today's politics. Recognizing moments in history that sparked unity can inspire today's voters. The struggle for Civil Rights in the 1960s serves as a poignant example. Today we are united by a common interest, Jobs, taxes, the high cost of food, our children's future in this country, and the Democratic Party's immigration policy. These are the common issues we share that should forever unite us and once united we should never go back.

The Journey Ahead

The journey toward a more unified political climate necessitates deliberate actions from every individual. It calls for patience, open-mindedness, and a sincere commitment to engaging in and contemplating challenging discussions. By actively participating in the electoral process, each voter plays a crucial role in crafting a political landscape that embraces collaboration rather than division. While our differences may be profoundly embedded, there remains an ever-present potential for growth and enhancement.

Encouraging Civic Engagement

We need civic engagement and civil discourse. We should come together and volunteer for local campaigns, participate in voter registration drives, or simply discuss important issues together. All of us play a role in shaping the political climate, and our actions can spark broader movements that challenge the status quo.

By stepping out of our comfort zones, we can inspire others to join the cause that will create a ripple effect of positive change. Grassroots efforts, community organizing, and educational initiatives can pave the way for a more inclusive political system. As we work to bridge gaps and promote understanding, we lay the groundwork for our future generations to inherit a more balanced democracy where collaboration triumphs over discord. We owe it to our children.

The Journey of Voting for Black Americans in America:

The journey of Black Americans in the United States is a long and profound one, starting well before the Civil War of 1865. To understand this history, we need to go back to the time when African people were brought to America against their will. They were forced into slavery, and this institution played a significant role in shaping the nation. The Transatlantic Slave Trade transported millions of Africans to America, where they were sold in markets and forced to work in harsh conditions on plantations, particularly in the South.

Chapter 7

The Democratic Party's Disdain For Black Americans

Slavery and Its Impact

While some don't want to hear this story, it's important to understand why voting is so important to Black Americans today because of what happened to their African American ancestors. Slavery lasted for more than two centuries in America. It created a system of oppression that affected generations of Black Americans. Enslaved people had no rights.

They weren't allowed to read or write, which prevented them from gaining knowledge that could help them fight for their freedom. However, many enslaved individuals resisted in various ways, such as working slowly, sabotaging equipment, or even escaping to freedom. The Underground Railroad, a network of secret routes and safe houses, emerged as a way for enslaved people to find their way to the North, where they could live free.

The Road to Freedom

The Civil War, which began in 1861, was a pivotal moment in American history. It was fought between the Northern states, known as the Union, and the Southern states, known as the Confederacy which was a part of the Democratic Party. A key issue at stake was slavery. The Union aimed to end the spread of slavery, while the Confederacy wanted to keep it. The war concluded in 1865 with the Union's victory, leading to the Emancipation Proclamation, which declared that all enslaved persons in the Confederate states were to be set free. Although this was a momentous step, the struggle for equality did not end there.

Reconstruction Era

Following the Civil War, the Reconstruction Era began. During this time, efforts were made to integrate formerly enslaved people into society. The 13th Amendment was passed, which officially abolished slavery. Additionally, the 14th Amendment granted citizenship to anyone born in the United States, including former slaves. The 15th Amendment aimed to ensure that Black men could vote. However, these advancements faced severe backlash. Many Southern states and the Democratic Party enacted laws known as Jim Crow laws that enforced segregation and disenfranchised Black citizens. This led to a long period of inequality and discrimination.

AMENDMENT TO THE AMENDMENT

IN THE NATURE OF SUBSTITUTE TO H.R. 40

OFFERED BY MR. GOHMERT On page 9, after line 23,
insert the following and redesignate all that follows accordingly:
"

G) Whether the Democratic Party should be responsible for any compensation awarded since it is the only relevant entity in existence today that supported the institution of slavery. _This support includes but is not limited to, the following actions: Democratic Party Platforms in the 1800s that advocated for the institution of slavery; the Democratic Party leading a 75-calendar-day filibuster against the 1964 Civil Rights Act;_ a Member of the Democratic Party, Senator Robert Byrd from West Virginia—a known recruiter for the Ku Klux Klan— leading fellow Democrats in their opposition to civil rights for African-Americans; Democrat enactment and enforcement of Jim Crow laws and civil codes that forced segregation and restricted freedoms of Black Americans in the United States.

The Struggle for Civil Rights

The fight for civil rights continued into the 20th century. Organizations like the NAACP (National Association for the Advancement of Colored People) were established to fight for equal rights. The Harlem Renaissance was a cultural movement during the 1920s that highlighted African American art, music, and literature. Writers, musicians, and artists like Langston Hughes and Duke Ellington emerged, showcasing the richness of Black culture. Despite this progress, racial segregation and discrimination remained deeply rooted in society.

The Civil Rights Movement

In the 1950s and 1960s, there was a significant surge in civil rights activism. Influential figures such as Martin Luther King Jr. and Rosa

Parks emerged as iconic symbols of the movement. King championed nonviolent protest, famously delivering his "I Have a Dream" speech during the historic March on Washington in 1963. This era also brought about monumental legislation, including the Civil Rights Act of 1964. However, the Democratic Party opposed the bill which led to a 75-day calendar filibuster against the Act.

Although the Civil Rights Act of 1964 was designed to prohibit discrimination based on race, color, or religion, it fell short as Black Americans continued to grapple with equal employment opportunities, equitable wages, and adequate housing. This enduring inequality ultimately compelled President John F. Kennedy to sign an Executive Order on Affirmative Action in 1961, before the Civil Rights Act of 1965. While President Kennedy seemed to have signed the bill with benevolent intentions, believing it would eradicate the federal government's unjust labor practices against Black Americans was optimistic, especially in light of the opposition from radicals within his Democratic Party who aimed to undermine affirmative action laws that could benefit Black citizens.

Consequently, Affirmative Action did not genuinely advance the interests of Black Americans but instead cultivated division between Black and white citizens. When Affirmative Action was instituted in education to tackle the exclusion of Black students from colleges, the Democratic Party recognized that Black Americans were inadequate given their historical lack of access to quality education. The presumption that they could competently compete with peers who had received superior educational opportunities was misguided. Essentially, Affirmative Action emerged as a strategy crafted by the radical left within the Democratic Party to deepen the rift between Blacks and whites in America.

While I believe President John F. Kennedy sought to abolish racial segregation through the creation of numerous laws aimed at securing Black people the right to live in a free society alongside their counterparts, he faced considerable resistance from members of his Democratic party. The laws enacted under JFK were intended to safeguard and improve the well-being of Black Americans.

The Equal Employment Opportunity Commission (EEOC), another organization initiated by President Kennedy, was established to ensure that the laws he put in place for Black people were upheld; All of these laws were enforced not by the Democratic Party but by a Democratic President JFK and members of the Republican Party. They crafted these laws to protect and enhance the welfare of Black Americans, who had historically been targeted by the Confederate and Ku Klux Klan factions associated with the Democratic Party.

However, these laws often failed to benefit Black Americans, instead favoring minorities who immigrated to the U.S. after the Jim Crow era. Black Americans in this country do not even have a hate crime bill law on the books.

The laws that truly benefited Black Americans were implemented by radical Republicans, who made these statutes part of the Constitution: the 13th Amendment abolished slavery, the 14th Amendment granted equal protection and citizenship to Blacks, and the 15th Amendment extended the right to vote. All of these measures were championed by the Republican Party.

There was considerable pushback and resistance from the Ku Klux Klan and white supremacists who were a part of the Democratic Party, resulting in political violence at the polls. This resistance from Democrats ultimately led to the Voting Rights Act of 1965, designed to eliminate the barriers that obstructed Black Americans from exercising their right to vote. The Republican Party was instrumental in granting Black Americans their freedoms, civil liberties, and the right to vote. Meanwhile, the radical democrats, the Klu Klux Klan, and the confederates continued on their crusades working in other high governmental agencies throughout the country.

Despite legal advancements, Black Americans continued to face significant challenges. Issues such as systemic racism, economic inequality, and police brutality persisted. The radical Democrats, Ku Klux Klan, and Confederates and their opposition against Black Americans advanced and infiltrated all levels of government, industry, and corporations. However, throughout history, Black Americans have made remarkable contributions to various fields, including science, mathematics, sports, politics, and religion. I find myself questioning why Black Americans maintain such unwavering loyalty to a party that hasn't demonstrated a commitment to resolving the issue they've faced for generations.

Chapter 8

Education is the Game Changer

Education has always been a crucial part of the Black American experience. Historically, access to quality education was restricted due to segregation. However, the establishment of Historically Black Colleges and Universities (HBCUs) created opportunities for Black students to pursue higher education. Today, these institutions continue to play a vital role in promoting academic excellence and community development.

In local communities across the nation, initiatives focusing on education, mentorship, and economic empowerment are becoming increasingly important. Since its inception, education in Black American communities has often underperformed and lacked the necessary resources to provide a quality education that allows us to compete with our peers. A quality education eliminates the need for affirmative action because everyone can compete on equal footing. Programs that encourage youth to engage in education and community service help build a brighter future. Education is the game changer. By empowering the next generation, we can reduce reliance on welfare programs and unintended pregnancies, prioritize family, and embrace the Black conservatism we've always been.

It was only after confronting numerous adversities, obstacles, and overt racism in New York that I felt an urgent need to grasp the true essence of the Democratic Party and the constituents it represented. Throughout my life, I had been led to believe that the Democratic Party championed the cause of the poor, the unjust, particularly the "Black" community. Yet, within a Democratic stronghold, I found myself facing resistance at every turn. This is what prompted me to delve deeply into the origins and objectives of the Democratic Party. What I uncovered left me profoundly unsettled; I was astounded. The realization that the very party I had steadfastly supported, advocated for, and defended throughout my adulthood was the same entity that had systematically marginalized and discriminated against me due to my race left me mortified.

My profound understanding of the history of the Democratic Party reveals their commitment to keeping Black Americans marginalized. This has been evident through their refusal to provide adequate protection, implement essential resources in our neighborhoods, and ensure a quality education across Black communities that would enable them to thrive. Furthermore, the creation of racially discriminatory laws, such as Jim Crow and others, highlights the systemic oppression enacted by this party. With this knowledge, I cannot, in good conscience, support a system that has perpetuated racist ideologies against a group of people, wielding their power to hinder Black Americans from achieving economic prosperity.

For far too long, Black Americans have participated in the electoral process, casting votes for candidates at every level, from local offices to the highest echelons of government. We have tirelessly supported our Black elected officials, yet they have largely profited at our expense. We have placed them in positions of power with the expectation that they would advocate for us by revitalizing the struggling communities they pledged to restore upon taking office.

They promised to combat the deterioration of our neighborhoods, but all we have received in return are hollow assurances while they amass wealth while in office. Over the past sixty years, we have continued to vote to keep these officials in power, and for sixty years, they have failed to address the socio-economic challenges faced by Black individuals in this nation. It is an utter disgrace.

I observe the dire public health crisis on Harlem's 125th Street, and the silence surrounding it is deafening. This is a Democratic state across the board, yet not one elected official has addressed the rampant addiction issues that plague Black communities in Harlem, New York. They are referred to as the "Walking Dead."

New York City has shuttered mental health facilities, drug rehabilitation centers, Alcoholics Anonymous programs, and other vital health services, leaving individuals to roam the streets aimlessly without support. The city faces a significant public health crisis that Democratic officials have chosen to ignore. The scene resembles something out of a horror film, and even citizens who are not directly impacted are affected indirectly. Why? Because these individuals require assistance that we, as individuals, are unable to provide. Moreover, there is a justified fear of being harmed by those who are so mentally compromised that they cannot fathom their own actions.

This ongoing crisis deteriorates our neighborhoods, discourages children from playing outside, and, most importantly, dehumanizes those in crisis, treating them as pariahs rather than individuals in need of compassion and support.

Not one Black celebrity has come forward to say, "What can be done to help". Not one Black elected official in a Democratic-run state, from top to bottom, has taken the crisis in Harlem, New York, seriously. This crisis hasn't just arisen; it has been ongoing for over twenty years. The health disparity for Black residents is deteriorating, the area has declined, and conditions are worsening. This is a profound disappointment.

In every Democratic-run state, Black communities and neighborhoods are in disarray. They often consist of projects, run-down homes, or deteriorating buildings, surrounded by liquor stores and little else. In these Democratic-run states, Black Americans resemble life on a slave plantation. The neighborhoods, communities, and spaces are in deplorable conditions. There are no educational resources to empower Black individuals to progress.

These are the Democratic-run states where Black individuals have consistently voted Democrat at a rate of 95% for over sixty years. Black individuals are not seeking handouts; we desire support from those we have elected to office. We are looking for backing from the very people we helped to elevate to prominence. We are not asking for cash directly; access to quality education and the establishment of excellent schools in Black neighborhoods is more than enough.

I have reflected on this many times, and perhaps now you should too: why were Black people killed for learning to read? Why have Black American communities, for so many decades, been home to the worst school systems in the country? If the Department of Education is responsible for public schools, why aren't there newly constructed, technologically advanced, high-quality schools in Black communities across America? My philosophy is this: show me someone in the DOJ who genuinely cares about the quality of education for all children, and I will show you children who can and will thrive. As previously stated, a quality education is a game changer.

Furthermore, regarding educational resources in Black neighborhoods, Democrats often profess to care about reproductive rights for women, but where are the women's health facilities in Black communities? Centers like breastfeeding centers, health clinics, and places where young girls facing unintended pregnancies can find support, such as childcare resources and free tuition to help them build a future for themselves and their children.

What about prenatal classes, prenatal yoga, wellness centers, and nutrition education centers? Where are the Democratic Party"s resources that promote families? These types of resources can equip families, particularly young girls with unintended pregnancies, helping them understand that they have choices that do not necessarily include terminating the pregnancy. Why not put resources in their communities that promote families, and education, that leads to prosperity? Reproductive rights are God-given.

What about resources for young boys, such as spaces for study and tutoring assistance? The Boys Club, established by three Republican women to provide a haven for young boys to engage in productive activities, has long since disappeared. It has been replaced by costly YMCAs catering to affluent families who can afford the steep monthly membership fees. Where are Black American tax dollars going? The only time young Black boys receive national attention is when scouts come into the neighborhoods to select an estimated twenty Black boys to play in professional sports. Twenty! Where are the fellowship achievement programs for low-middle-income Black and White boys? We can and should be doing so much more.

Creating Safe Spaces for Inner-City Youth

Professional ball players have the potential to have a significant impact on the lives of inner-city Black boys. They can provide these young individuals with a safe place to escape the challenges of their neighborhoods. Many of these neighborhoods are plagued by issues like gun violence, which can create a sense of hopelessness. By offering mentorship and support, athletes can help boys explore their options and aspirations. It is vital to show them that there are paths in life that do not lead to violence or crime.

For example, setting up local sports camps can be an effective way for athletes to engage with youth. These camps can teach not just sports skills but also life skills. The training they receive can instill a sense of discipline, teamwork, and determination. Moreover, inviting guest speakers or role models to share their stories can inspire these boys to dream bigger. They need to see successful people who have faced similar challenges and have made positive choices in their lives. These Black boys need role models, and father figures.

The Role of Music in Education

The MTV Save the Music fellowship program is another example of how we can support inner-city youth. This program takes students to hear live orchestras, exposing them to the beauty of music. It also helps schools by donating musical instruments. Music education has proven benefits, such as improving academic performance and enhancing social skills. It allows kids to express themselves and find a passion that could steer them away from negative influences.

To build on this idea, schools can develop after-school music programs that are accessible to all children, regardless of their background. For instance, schools could host regular musical workshops where students can learn to play different instruments. They can also include vocal training and music theory in the curriculum. Such initiatives require funding and support from the community. Local businesses, parents, and organizations can collaborate to raise money and resources for these programs, fostering a sense of collective responsibility for the youth's education.

Investing in Our Children

It is essential to shift our focus from issues like illegal immigration to investing in our own children, especially those from low and middle-income backgrounds, whether they are Black or White. Investing in youth means creating opportunities for growth and development. This investment can come in many forms, including education, job training, and community programs.

For instance, establishing summer job programs can provide young people with valuable work experience. These programs can teach them essential skills that prepare them for future employment. Local businesses can partner with schools to offer internships or job shadowing opportunities. This exposure helps kids understand the working world and what it takes to succeed in various careers.

Focusing on Family

Ensuring productive lives for young people first requires a family-first approach. Families play a crucial role in a child's development. They provide the support system needed for children to thrive. Therefore, it is vital to invest in family services that promote parental education and resource access. Communities can organize workshops focusing on parenting skills, financial literacy, and mental health resources.

For example, community centers can host meetings to discuss issues like effective communication within families or managing household stress. They might also offer resources for counseling or family therapy. By supporting families, we empower them to better nurture their children, ultimately leading to improved outcomes for the next generation.

The Importance of Community Involvement

As we consider what we should be voting for, it is important to reflect on the role of community involvement. Local communities can take a stand by creating programs that appeal to youth. Churches, schools, and non-profit organizations can come together to provide safe recreational spaces, educational resources, and mentorship opportunities. I know so many women preachers who are very well-educated. Female pastors, the community needs your support to teach and educate kids in the communities. We need you to step down from the pulpit, and be of service to your community as God would want it.

How about setting up community gardens that teach kids about healthy eating and responsibility? These gardens could also serve as a gathering place for families, enhancing community bonds. Furthermore, organizing neighborhood clean-up days can instill a sense of pride in one's surroundings. Engaging youth in these types of activities helps them feel valued and part of something larger than themselves.

Bringing Back Trade Schools

Trade schools have become an important topic of discussion in recent years. There is a growing recognition that not everyone is suited to go to college. While higher education offers valuable opportunities for many, trade schools provide a practical alternative for individuals who want to acquire specific skills without pursuing a traditional four-year degree. These schools focus on hands-on training that prepares students for careers in various fields, such as construction, plumbing, electrical work, and healthcare.

Importance of Trade Schools

Trade schools can serve as a vital resource for those who desire to support a family without attending college. Many students finish high school and are unsure about their next steps. For some, the idea of accumulating student debt to attend a university is daunting. Trade schools offer a more feasible option, allowing students to learn the skills they need to enter the workforce quickly. These programs typically last from a few months to a couple of years, enabling students to enter their chosen fields sooner than traditional college graduates.

In addition to being cost-effective, trade schools provide the opportunity to learn valuable skills that are in high demand. For instance, skilled trades such as welding, carpentry, and home health care are essential, and the demand for qualified workers continues to grow. Students who pursue these fields can find stable employment, often with good salaries.

For example, a licensed electrician can earn a competitive wage, allowing them to support a family while also building a rewarding career.

Benefits of Vocational Training

Vocational training goes beyond just learning a trade; it also equips students with essential life skills. These schools often incorporate lessons on business practices, safety regulations, and customer service. For instance, a heating and cooling technician not only learns the technical aspects of the job but also how to communicate effectively with clients. This blend of technical and soft skills is essential for success in any career.

Furthermore, trade schools often have partnerships with local businesses. This connection allows students to gain real-world experience through internships or apprenticeships. Such experiences can lead to job offers even before graduation, significantly easing the transition from school to work. For example, a student enrolled in a culinary program might have the chance to intern at a local restaurant, which could lead to employment once they complete their training.

Supporting Families through Trade Skills

One of the most compelling reasons to promote trade schools is the positive impact they can have on families and communities. Graduates of trade programs can secure well-paying jobs, which contribute to economic stability. When individuals have access to good-paying employment, they can provide for their families, invest in their children's education, and contribute to their communities. This can create a cycle of prosperity that benefits everyone.

By bringing back trade schools, we create pathways for individuals to enter the workforce and fulfill their career aspirations. Many parents want to set an example for their children by demonstrating the value of hard work and self-sufficiency. By pursuing a trade, they can show their kids that there are many paths to success. This can inspire younger generations to think about their futures and consider options beyond a traditional college education.

Making Trade Schools Accessible

To make trade schools more appealing, it is essential to ensure accessibility for all students. This includes providing financial aid or scholarships to help cover tuition costs. Many potential students may shy away from vocational training due to financial constraints, so having resources available is crucial. Additionally, schools can develop outreach programs in high schools to raise awareness about the opportunities available in trade fields. Outreach programs in high schools are imperative because they provide students with other professionals out there that they may have an interest in for example, so many students would like to be referees in sports, airline pilots, meteorologists, farmers, etc. when you bring awareness and provide pathways that's how students succeed.

Encouraging Lifelong Learning

Lastly, trade schools should embrace the concept of lifelong learning. Once students complete their training and enter the workforce, they should have opportunities to continue their education. This could involve offering refresher courses, advanced certifications, or workshops to stay updated on industry standards. For instance, a mechanic might benefit from periodic training on the latest automotive technology, allowing them to remain competitive in the field.

Lifelong learning also encourages adaptability. We live in a fast-paced world, where industries change rapidly. If we foster a culture of continuous education, trade schools can help graduates stay relevant and ready to tackle new challenges. This approach not only supports individual careers but also strengthens entire industries.

By bringing back trade schools, we can provide a viable alternative to traditional college education. These institutions will prepare students for stable, fulfilling careers that allow them to support their families and contribute to their communities. With the right support and resources, trade schools can play a vital role in shaping the future workforce and driving economic growth.

Modernizing the Curriculum

One important aspect of education today is modernizing the curriculum to better reflect what is happening in the job market. The job market is always changing because technology keeps evolving. This means the skills that employers are looking for can shift quickly. By incorporating training in these new technologies, educational programs can remain relevant and appealing to students.

Relevance of New Technologies

Training in advanced manufacturing is another critical piece of the puzzle. This includes the use of automation, robotics, and smart manufacturing systems. For instance, students learning about robotics might work with programmable robots to understand how they operate in a factory setting. This kind of hands-on experience can be incredibly valuable. It not only helps students learn but also makes them more attractive to potential employers who are looking for these types of workers with practical skills.

Making the curriculum relevant is essential because it attracts more students. When students see that their education is aligned with the skills needed in the workforce, they are more likely to be engaged and excited about learning. Schools that adapt their programs to include modern technologies can create a more fulfilling learning environment.

Accessibility of Training Programs

To further this idea, schools should aim to make some of this training and these trade programs accessible during the last two years of high school. This is a crucial time for students as they prepare to leave school and enter the workforce. Offering programs that expose students to various trades and technologies can help them feel ready for life after graduation.

Imagine a high school where students can take courses in fields like electrical work, plumbing, or even coding. These programs should be designed to give students a basic understanding, along with the chance to get practical experience. For instance, a class on computer programming could include projects where students develop their own simple applications. This real-world application reinforces learning and helps students build a portfolio to show future employers.

Transitioning to the Workforce

Another effective idea is to create partnerships with local businesses. Schools could work with companies to provide internships or on-the-job training experiences. For instance, train students in nursing during their last two years of high school, and then after graduation they will intern at a hospital for two years with a paid stipend, upon completing the internship they will be tested to become registered and start their career as a registered nurse.

The Importance of Internships

Internships are an invaluable part of this transition. They allow students to apply what they have learned in the classroom to real-life situations. An internship can include shadowing a mentor, working on projects, or attending meetings. This environment encourages students to ask questions and learn from experienced professionals.

Moreover, internships can often lead to job offers after graduation. When a student proves to be reliable and skilled during their internship, companies may want to bring them on as full-time employees. This transition from school to work can be smoother when students have these kinds of opportunities available to them.

Building Career Skills

It's also important to teach students about soft skills along with technical skills. Soft skills include teamwork, communication, problem-solving, and time management. These skills are essential in almost every job and can sometimes be just as important as technical abilities. Schools can incorporate lessons and activities that help build these skills.

For example, group projects can teach students how to work together and communicate effectively. Workshops on resume writing and interview techniques can prepare students for job applications. Role-playing scenarios can provide practice for handling difficult situations in the workplace.

As technology continues to advance, the job market is likely to change even more. Therefore, keeping the curriculum up to date is a never-ending task. Schools must continually assess the needs of local industries and adjust their programs accordingly. By doing so, they can ensure that students are equipped with the most relevant skills and knowledge. Students of every race Black and White need to be better prepared for the future.

Programs that bridge the gap between education and employment will create a more skilled and adaptable workforce. When students feel confident in their abilities and prepared for their careers, it benefits everyone in the community. Employers gain dedicated workers, and students build successful careers. This cycle of education and practical training continues to strengthen the job market for all of us.

Reevaluating Our Priorities

It is essential to reevaluate where our priorities lie. Focusing on our youth and their futures could bring about lasting change. Instead of just discussing problems, we need to explore concrete solutions. We should champion programs that uplift children and leverage the wealth of resources available in our communities.

Whether it's through sports, music, family programs, or community initiatives, the goal should be to create a supportive environment that fosters growth. By standing together as a community, with our tax dollars going back into our communities and schools, we can ensure that children have the opportunities they need to thrive. It is our collective responsibility to give them the tools necessary for success and to encourage them to aspire for more without falling into the traps that so often claim their peers.

The Impact on the Job Market

When our children are educated and trained, they enter the job market with skills that employers value. This means more people are employed in skilled positions, contributing to a thriving economy. As everyone finds meaningful work, they earn good salaries, which helps to improve living standards. A stable job market encourages spending, stimulates growth, and promotes innovation. When the economy thrives, we see a reduction in unemployment and an increase in opportunities. This cycle of education, training, and employment builds a strong foundation for society.

Chapter 9

Americans First/ Then Legal Immigrants

Once we have educated our children and ensured they are prepared for skilled jobs, we come to the topic of immigration. There will inevitably be a need for labor in unskilled positions. This is where legal immigration can play a vital role. Bringing in individuals who are legally allowed to work helps fill these roles. **This process should occur after we have prioritized our own American Citizens and their education. It ensures that the job market has been assessed and that there is a need for additional workers.**

Filling Unskilled Labor Gaps

The reason for focusing on the need for unskilled labor becomes clear when we consider the workforce landscape. *With our children successfully occupying skilled jobs,* we may find gaps in areas that require unskilled labor. Examples of unskilled jobs include positions in agriculture, hospitality, and fast-food restaurants. These roles are often essential for the functioning of many industries. By bringing in legal immigrants to fill these jobs, where we are not taking opportunities away from American citizens. Instead, we are supporting the economy by ensuring that all roles are filled efficiently.

Protecting American Workers

By prioritizing the education and training of American youth, you create a system where immigration complements our existing workforce rather than competes with it. This approach protects American workers, as it focuses on developing homegrown talent first. When families are taken care of, and children enter the job market with skills, we create a healthy balance between skilled and unskilled positions. It encourages a thriving job market where everyone has a chance to contribute and succeed.

Supporting Family First Policies

Policies that support families should be a priority. This includes access to free childcare, healthcare, and educational resources. When families can thrive, the benefits extend into the community and the overall economy. Investing in our families helps to ensure that our children grow up with the necessary support and resources. Lawmakers must recognize the importance of family-first policies as they contribute to building a better future for our children.

Building a Sustainable Economy

A well-educated workforce is the backbone of a sustainable economy. By training our children and ensuring they have opportunities, we create a system that promotes growth and innovation. When our citizens are employed and flourishing, we build a stable economy. This stability allows for investment and development that can further elevate our society. The cycle of education, job placement, and economic growth is vital to maintaining balance within our nation.

Helpful government involvement

Government involvement is also important in this process. Parents, schools, and local organizations must collaborate to ensure that children have access to the best possible education and training. By working together, we can create programs that serve the needs of students and families. Community engagement ensures that children are supported and that families know they are a priority. Events, workshops, and ongoing communication between families and schools can foster a sense of belonging, ultimately benefiting everyone involved.

A Balanced Approach

By taking care of our families first, through education and vocational training, we create an environment where both skilled and unskilled labor needs are met. Our children can thrive in the job market, and any necessary legal immigration can occur without displacing American workers. This thoughtful, balanced approach ensures that our economy remains strong while supporting the lives of our citizens and newcomers alike. America has to prioritize its citizens and work together to create a healthy country rather than a divisive one.

When students graduate from high school with real-world experience and connections, they are better equipped for the job market. They can enter positions with confidence, aware that they possess practical knowledge and experience. This benefits not only the students but also local businesses by supplying them with skilled workers prepared to contribute.

Americans are investing in the jobs they desire instead of being trained and educated for the positions that need to be filled, and the cost is excessive, leaving Americans in significant debt with no return on their investment.

Putting Citizens First in Elections

When America prioritizes its citizens, it creates a more effective and fair election process. This means ensuring that every individual has a voice and can participate in shaping their government. When citizens feel valued, they engage more actively in the democratic process. When candidates come out to the community and speak with us and address our concerns is important. Their participation can lead to outcomes that reflect the true needs and desires of the community.

Importance of Citizen Engagement

Citizen engagement is crucial in any democracy. Engaging with voters involves more than just encouraging them to cast their ballots. It requires a commitment from leaders to listen to the concerns of the people. For example, a community meeting can be a great way to bring citizens together to discuss local issues. We're not looking for the candidates to bring in their representatives, we want to speak with the candidate directly. If local leaders hold these meetings regularly, they can gather valuable input from residents. This input helps shape policies that address actual community needs, resulting in a more representative government.

Transparency in the Voting Process

Chapter 10

Democracy

What Does Democracy Mean Today?

To clarify, we should examine what democracy means today compared to the past. At its core, democracy is about the involvement of citizens in their government. It enables individuals to express their opinions, vote in elections, and hold their leaders accountable. For instance, participating in local elections, town hall meetings, or rallies can empower citizens to influence policies that impact their lives.

The media has become biased and prevents fair political discourse from both sides which has created hostility and division among voters. The media's bias has turned into nothing more than destructive rhetoric. We the people need the media and journalists to understand constructive dialogue between two candidates fosters understanding and cooperation, while destructive rhetoric only leads to mistrust and polarization.

The Historical Context of Democracy

Understanding the historical context of democracy is vital. In the early days of the United States, democracy meant limited participation; not everyone had the right to vote. Over time, civil rights movements expanded access to voting, and the definition of democracy grew to

Another important aspect of putting citizens first is maintaining a transparent voting system. Voters need to understand how their votes are counted and what measures are in place to ensure that elections are fair. For instance, using technology to track ballots can help reassure citizens that their votes are secure. Public demonstrations of the voting process can also foster trust among voters. When people know that there is transparency, they are more likely to participate in elections. Voting in America's Presidential elections is granted to United States Citizens.

Accessibility of Voting

Ensuring that voting is accessible to everyone is also key to putting citizens first. This includes making polling places available in various locations and ensuring they are open to all individuals, including those with disabilities. States can also implement early voting to make it easier for people who cannot vote on Election Day. Abiding by the same rules such as ID requirements should remain the same. Additionally, mail-in ballots can help those who may face challenges getting to a voting location. Providing clear information on how to register and vote is equally essential.

Educating Citizens about the Election Process

Education plays a significant role in the engagement of citizens. If individuals are not informed about when and how to vote, they may miss the opportunity to take part in elections. School programs and community workshops can educate people about the voting process. Tutorials on how to fill out ballots correctly can also minimize potential mistakes that could disenfranchise voters. Information should be easily accessible, perhaps through websites or local offices, so everyone can find out what they need.

Championing Diverse Voices

While America is a melting pot of cultures and backgrounds, it is essential to ensure that the voices of low- and middle-class Black and White voters are heard. Therefore, it is necessary to uphold fairness by preventing politicians from Black foreign nations from voting on policies that affect Black Americans. The rationale behind this is that many Black foreigners come to America primarily for work. The overwhelming majority of Black foreigners often do not seek to understand the historical oppression faced by Black Americans in this country. Additionally, our cultures differ significantly; Black Americans tend to prioritize family structures such as marriage and parenting, and they uphold beliefs in gender roles and spirituality. Generally, Black Americans adopt a more conservative perspective. There is a clear difference in beliefs between the two groups, and Black foreigners often do not connect with the history of Black Americans or their way of life. It would be unjust for Black foreigners to assume political office and make decisions about a group of people they do not fully understand or regard as a problem.

Building Trust in Political Institutions

To put citizens first, it is essential to build trust in political institutions. If individuals feel that their government does not represent their interests or is not acting in good faith, they may hesitate to participate in elections. Unfortunately, there has been a lot of mistrust in the political institutions.

Americans have borne witness to a lot of lies on the campaign trials and have witnessed a lot of media bias that we feel brings corruption to the entire political process. Americans believe that elected officials and political parties rebuild this trust by maintaining honesty and integrity in their actions. Regularly engaging with constituents through town halls or social media can also enhance transparency, fostering a greater sense of trust among citizens.

Utilizing Technology for Engagement

Technology can be a powerful tool for engaging citizens in the electoral process. Social media platforms can be utilized to spread information about elections, remind people about voting days, and share important updates. Additionally, mobile apps can help people learn more about the candidates and issues on the ballot. By integrating technology into the voting process, it becomes easier for younger generations to engage, thus encouraging broader participation.

However, young voters who aren't engaged will need a reason to become engaged, and explaining to them that it's their civic duty will not be enough. To successfully engage young voters, the messages delivered must resonate with their experiences and concerns. This means understanding the issues that are important to them. For example, many young people are anxious about student debt, and job opportunities, Campaigns that address these issues directly and not gaslight the issue, can capture their interest. By framing voting as a way to have a say in these matters, young voters may feel more inclined to participate

Creating a Positive Voting Experience

Making the voting experience positive is another way to put citizens first. Long lines, confusing ballots, and unfriendly poll workers can discourage people from voting. Streamlined processes can improve the overall experience. This can include better training for poll workers or using efficient technology to speed up check-in and ballot casting. When the process is user-friendly, people are more likely to return to vote in future elections.

Engaging Youth in the Process

Engaging young people in the electoral process is particularly important for the health of democracy. Young voters often have different priorities and perspectives. Initiatives like voter registration drives at high schools and colleges can help empower them. By involving youth in discussions about issues that affect them, leaders can cultivate a lifelong habit of civic engagement. Encouraging young people to take an interest in elections can lead to a more connected and informed generation if the outcome of voting is more inclined to address their concerns. Again, I don't see this generation constantly voting on the same issues where they see no resolution

Recognizing the Role of Community Leaders

Community leaders also play a significant role in putting citizens first in elections. They can serve as bridges to connect the government with the people. By advocating for the community's needs and voicing concerns, these leaders can ensure that the issues affecting residents are addressed in the electoral process. Local influencers can help mobilize groups and motivate them to participate in elections, reinforcing the importance of citizen engagement.

Promoting Vote-by-Mail Options

Vote-by-mail options is something I see would be extremely popular among young voters. Many people find it easier to fill out their ballots at home, away from the rush of polling places. By promoting and facilitating vote-by-mail options, states can increase the overall turnout. Clear instructions should accompany mail-in ballots to minimize confusion and ensure that votes are counted correctly.

Fostering a Culture of Participation

Fostering a culture of participation goes beyond just voting. It involves encouraging citizens to remain engaged in their communities throughout the year, not just during election seasons. Local events, forums, and discussions help build connections between citizens and public officials. The more engaged people are, and the more elected officials are meeting the needs of these young voters, the more they will feel invested in the electoral process and the outcomes of elections.

The recent generations, particularly Millennials and Generation Z, are known for their intelligence and awareness. They have grown up in an age where information is readily available at their fingertips. This access to knowledge has made them more discerning. They can quickly spot when someone is trying to deceive them or when something does not add up. This generation values authenticity and transparency. For instance, they might research candidates extensively before voting. A simple slogan or flashy campaign is no longer enough to win their support.

A Demand for Honesty

These younger voters have little patience for dishonesty. They can identify when someone is trying to manipulate them or offer vague promises. For example, if a politician makes ambitious claims but does not provide details on how they will achieve them, these generations will likely respond with skepticism. They expect candidates to present concrete plans. The voters want to know the steps that will be taken to implement these plans.

The Importance of Earning Trust

When it comes to earning the votes of these generations, candidates must build trust. Trust can be built through consistency and honesty in communication. This means that if someone in a position of power identifies an issue, they must address it directly and take action. For example, if a leader sees a pressing problem in their community, they should outline their plans to tackle it rather than divert attention elsewhere. By doing so, they demonstrate that they are taking their constituents seriously.

Being Authentic

Being authentic goes beyond just honesty; it includes being relatable. Younger generations appreciate when leaders share personal stories or experiences. This relatability helps create a connection. For instance, if a politician discusses their own struggles with education or housing, it makes them more human. They become someone the voters can relate to, rather than just a distant figure. Authenticity can make a significant impact on how voters perceive a candidate.

A Shift in Expectations

The expectations held by these generations have shifted dramatically compared to previous ones. Older generations might have accepted vague assurances without much questioning. However, Millennials and Gen Z expect tangible results. They want to see measurable outcomes from policies and programs. They are not impressed by grand speeches but rather by what changes actually occur. For instance, if a new policy is introduced to improve education, these voters will be looking for data showing improvements in student outcomes.

The Power of Social Media

Social media plays a significant role in how these generations engage with political figures. Platforms like Twitter, Instagram, and TikTok are powerful tools for communication. Politicians who use these platforms effectively can connect directly with young voters. However, the same platforms can also expose dishonesty quickly. A poorly thought-out comment or a misleading post can lead to backlash almost immediately. Candidates need to be mindful of their online presence and how it affects their reputation.

Preparedness for Debate

Debates and public discussions have become pivotal moments in elections. Younger voters pay close attention to how candidates respond to tough questions. If someone tries to evade a question or offers a vague answer, it often leads to a loss of respect. These generations want to see candidates who are prepared to discuss their views openly. This preparation shows that they take the issues seriously. Therefore, candidates should practice addressing difficult topics head-on.

Advocacy for Issues

Younger generations are also more likely to support candidates who champion specific issues. They tend to care deeply about social justice, and equality. Advocating for clear, actionable changes can create a sense of alignment with values that matter to these demographics.

Navigating Challenges

Politicians often face various challenges when trying to engage younger voters. One significant issue is the overwhelming amount of information they are exposed to. In a world filled with noise, standing out is difficult. Therefore, candidates need to communicate clearly and consistently. Mixing humor, facts, and a genuine approach can help grab attention while maintaining credibility.

Accountability is Key

Accountability is an increasingly important concept for these voters. If a politician makes promises, they will be held responsible for following through. These generations expect transparency in governance and will demand answers if expectations are not met. For example, if a law is passed to improve public transport, these voters will look for updates on its implementation and effectiveness.

Building Community Connections

Engagement should also focus on building community connections. Organizing events that allow for face-to-face interactions can create a more personal relationship between politicians and voters. Creating safe spaces where people feel heard encourages dialogue. When younger generations see that their thoughts and opinions are valued, they are more likely to support those who listen.

Ultimately, the future of politics hinges on understanding these new generations. Recognizing their intelligence and concern for authenticity is crucial. Politicians must adapt to this landscape by prioritizing honesty, relatability, and issue advocacy. By doing so, they can earn the respect and trust of Millennials and Generation Z, ensuring their voices are truly represented in the political arena.

The Growing Awareness of Recent Generations

Recent generations, particularly Millennials and Generation Z, are recognized for their keen intelligence and high level of awareness. They have experienced life in a unique environment where information is always just a click away. This constant access to knowledge shapes the way they view the world. They can quickly discern falsehoods and recognize when something isn't quite right. This critical thinking is a valuable skill in a society filled with misinformation.

Valuing Authenticity and Transparency

One significant trait of these generations is their strong preference for authenticity and transparency. They are not easily swayed by superficial approaches. For example, when it comes to voting, they tend to conduct thorough research on candidates and issues. This means that they look beyond catchy slogans or flashy ads. Instead, they want to understand the individuals behind the campaigns and the values they represent. They examine voting records, public statements, and even the candidates' histories to ensure that they align with their beliefs.

Researching Candidates

For those seeking to engage with Millennials and Gen Z voters, it is vital to provide clear, factual information. They might review a candidate's website, look for external news articles, and even check social media for public opinions. This means that candidates need to ensure that their messaging is consistent and transparent across all platforms. Genuinely engaging with voters—answering questions and actively participating in discussions—can significantly impact how they are perceived.

The Demographics

In terms of numbers, Millennials, born between 1981 and 1996, comprise approximately 72.7 million individuals in the U.S. This makes them the largest generational group in the country. On the other hand, Generation Z consists of those born between 1997 and 2012, totaling about 69 million people. This combination means that together, these two generations represent roughly 48% of the U.S. population. Their sheer size means they hold considerable influence over social, political, and cultural landscapes.

Implications for the Future

Given their awareness and ability to see through deception, there are important implications for the future of voting in America. Traditional methods of persuasion may not work as effectively as they once did. For instance, candidates who rely solely on charisma or empty promises may find themselves losing support. Instead, they need to present real solutions and evidence of their capabilities.

Social Issues and Voting Behavior

Another critical consideration is the current social issues that resonate with these generations. Topics such as climate social justice, and economic inequality are particularly significant to them. They are more likely to support candidates who prioritize these issues and demonstrate a commitment to addressing them. The call for change and action creates an environment where straightforward, honest communication is appreciated.

Engaging with Issues

Candidates aiming to resonate with these voters must demonstrate genuine engagement with these pressing issues. This involves articulating specific policies and detailing their implementation plans. For example, offering free education to prepare individuals for high-paying skilled job vacancies is essential; thus, candidates must be ready to deliver, as these generations will not grant candidates a second chance. First impression is everything.

The Challenge of Gaslighting

The concept of gaslighting—a form of manipulation that causes someone to question their sanity or perception of reality—does not work well in these generations. They are accustomed to seeking out facts and rejecting the misleading narratives that often circulate in political arenas. When they encounter attempts to mislead or manipulate them, they tend to push back. This power dynamic shifts the focus in political campaigns, forcing candidates to approach discussions and debates with authenticity and substance.

The Role of Media and Information

Moreover, the role of media and information dissemination plays a crucial part in shaping the perspectives of Millennials and Gen Z. With social media, online articles, and other digital platforms, they consume news differently than previous generations. They favor visual content, quick summaries, and real-time updates that allow them to stay informed. This indicates that candidates and political organizations must adapt their strategies to engage with these mediums effectively.

Bridging the Gap

To bridge the gap between generations, there needs to be an understanding of the unique perspectives that Millennials and Gen Z bring to the table. Engaging in conversations that matter to them, whether through social media campaigns, community events, or town hall meetings, is essential. These efforts reflect an understanding of their priorities and a willingness to listen.

Conclusion on a Commitment to Change

As the voting landscape continues to evolve, recognizing and responding to the characteristics of these generations becomes vital. Their intelligence, awareness, and strong desire for authenticity will shape how political candidates approach their campaigns. This generation's voice will not only influence future elections but also drive broader societal changes, making it crucial for all political entities to adapt their messages and strategies accordingly.

The Challenges of the New Generations

The government faces significant challenges today, especially with 48% of the American population being Millennials and Generation Z. These younger generations are known for their unique way of thinking. They are intellectual thinkers who value information and tend to question motives. They do not easily fall for traditional political tactics. Instead of sticking to one party for decades, they are more likely to change their minds based on how they feel about a candidate's actions. If they think a politician is being dishonest or manipulative, they will not hesitate to vote them out, even before their term ends. This shift in the political landscape is crucial for the government to understand.

The Political Landscape

With this demographic shift, the Democratic Party's recent immigration policies become clearer. Over the past three to four years, the party has brought in more than 20 million immigrants, including individuals from various backgrounds. The reasoning behind this influx seems to be tied to a need for more voters. This strategy aims to support the party's electoral base. However, Millennials and Generation Z will not blindly support the

Democrats simply because they happen to be Democrats. They seek authenticity and honesty in their leaders. They want to see real efforts being made to improve society rather than just promises.

Historical Context

Looking back to the early 1980s, we can find parallels between past events and current policies. During the CIA crack epidemic, which disproportionately affected Black Americans, there was also a significant influx of immigrants. This included people from places like Barbados, Jamaica, and Haiti. At that time, I was too young to grasp the complexities of these dynamics, but it became clear that the government needed to address its shortcomings. There was a crime epidemic, and the government was under intense scrutiny. They had to find a way to shift the focus away from their failures.

The Need for Workers and Voters

In addition to addressing the problems within the Black community, the government sought workers to fill job vacancies that were created during economic shifts. This need extended beyond just labor; it was also about securing a political future. New voters were essential for maintaining control. The influx of immigrant populations not only contributed to the workforce but also expanded the voting base. This relationship highlighted how political motives can shape immigration policies and how demographic changes can impact political landscapes.

The Demographic Breakdown

Currently, if Millennials and Generation Z make up 48% of the population, the remaining demographics consist of middle-aged individuals and older Americans. About 25% of the population falls into the middle-aged category, while the rest are seniors. Understanding this breakdown is crucial for policymakers. The perspectives of these different age groups vary widely, and what resonates with one generation may not with another.

Understanding the Young Electorate

The younger generations demand a new type of political engagement. They are not satisfied with the status quo and want to know what candidates will do about the pressing issues facing society today. For instance, Free education, high-salary paying jobs, and job security a significant concerns for many young voters. If politicians do not take these issues seriously, they will struggle to secure votes from these generations. Being genuine and transparent about policies is key to building trust with Millennials and Generation Z.

The Role of Transparency

Transparency in governance has never been more important. Young voters are adept at accessing information, and they often research candidates extensively before voting. They want to know about a candidate's past actions, proposed policies, and how these will affect their lives. This generation values honesty and can quickly identify when they are being misled. If they feel that a candidate is not sincere, they will likely choose not to support them, regardless of party affiliation

.

Younger generations are increasingly disinterested in the long-standing issues faced by their parents and grandparents. As baby boomers prepare for retirement and the next generation steps in, Millennials and Gen Z question why they must borrow money to secure jobs arising from retirement. Additionally, why are Americans taking loans from the government to fill public sector vacancies, only to face repayment periods of ten to twenty years? Would it not be more beneficial to implement work preparedness programs during high school, where students receive education and training, enabling them to graduate with the necessary skills to occupy these roles without the burden of student loan debt? Why is the situation structured this way?

Another significant issue expressed by the millennials and Gen Z is a frequently asked question on social media, which concerns government taxation of Americans. If Uncle Sam taxes their paychecks, how can it rationalize taxing them again on expenditures made from already-taxed income? This applies to routine purchases such as groceries, retail, dining, and more. Enough with the gaslighting.

Millennials and Gen Z, together, constitute an impressive 48% of America's population, representing a significant demographic that is shaping the future of the nation. This robust group is characterized by their desire for equity and a variety of investment opportunities that align with their values and aspirations. Recognizing the importance of authenticity in their interactions, they prioritize honesty and integrity, believing that one's word should be a binding commitment rather than a mere formality.

As these generations navigate the political landscape, they express a strong disinterest in conventional political maneuvers, particularly those that involve the influx of new illegal immigrants whenever a fresh cohort of Americans reaches voting age. Such tactics are seen as a response born out of fear rather than a genuine approach to the governance of Americans. Millennials and Gen Z call for authentic engagement and are eager for meaningful change that reflects their ideals and concerns. They advocate for policies that offer real solutions, promote social justice, and ensure that all voices are heard in the democratic process, seeking to build a future that resonates with their vision of equity and progress.

Democracy

Democracy is a term frequently used in America, but its meaning has shifted significantly throughout history. Originally, democracy was defined as "Of the people, by the people." This phrase embodies the idea that the government is created and maintained by the participation of its citizens. In the past, democracy carried a sense of trust and honor; it was a word that invoked respect and a belief in the power of the people. However, as time has passed, the term has become distorted.

The Changing Nature of the Term

Today, democracy often feels like a word that has lost its original strength. Many people use it so casually that they might not fully grasp its significance. It can sometimes seem overwhelming, or even frightening; it may feel almost like a swear word, given the context in which it's used. The phrase "a threat to our democracy" is a common example. This statement can provoke anxiety, and it raises questions about what democracy truly means in the current climate.

include a more diverse and inclusive population. The civil rights movement is an excellent example of how people have fought to redefine democracy to include more voices. These efforts have patched some of the gaps in representation, yet challenges persist.

The Weight of the Word

With the rapid transformation of society and technology, the weight of the word democracy may feel diminished. As people hear politicians and commentators reference democracy in various contexts, they may feel confused about its true meaning. Questions arise: Are we still aligned with the original principles? Is the concept of democracy still relevant? While the term may not carry the same gravity it once did, it is important to remember its foundational role in society.

The Impact of Language on Democracy

Language can influence people's understanding of democracy. Especially when you see powerful figures use the term to instill fear, it manipulates public perception. For example, by suggesting that democracy is under threat, they can rally support for policies that may not align with their ideals, which I guess is the point. This type of language acts as both a tool and a weapon. People must understand the essence of the word democracy so that they may guard themselves from being manipulated by thoughtless rhetoric.

Reclaiming the Essence of Democracy

To reclaim the true essence of democracy, We the people must hold institutions accountable for misinformation. We must educate ourselves about each candidate so that we don't rely on being misled and misinformed. We should start attending community meetings and engaging in discussions with our neighbors, this can foster a greater understanding of local issues.

Furthermore, we can take part in grassroots organizing. This can involve working with local advocacy groups on significant issues, such as education, healthcare, and safety. By getting involved, we not only learn more about democracy but we contribute to shaping the society we want to live in. If we work towards a shared understanding we can help rebuild the respect and honor democracy once stood for.

The Media is the fourth branch of the Government

The Role of Media in Government

Most people do not realize how much the media affects the government and our daily lives. The media is intended to serve as a bridge between the government and the public. It should provide information that helps citizens make informed choices. This connection is crucial in a democratic society because voters need to be well-informed to decide on important issues and candidates.

Media as the Fourth Branch of Government

Some people refer to the media as the fourth branch of government. This idea emphasizes the media's important role in checking and balancing the power of the other three branches: the executive, the legislative, and the judicial. Without a strong and functioning media, it is difficult for citizens to understand what is happening in their government. The media has a duty to report the facts, explain policies, and hold leaders accountable for their actions.

Responsibility to Inform Voters

The responsibility to inform voters is a significant part of what the media does. Journalists and news organizations should work hard to provide information on elections, policies, and social issues. They should aim to present facts clearly and accurately so that voters can grasp the complexities of what is happening in their government. For example, a news report about a new law should explain what the law entails, its potential impact on the community, and any debates around it. This helps voters understand the implications and make educated choices.

Holding Media Accountable

As citizens, we must hold the media accountable. This means we should demand fairness and objectivity in news reporting. If we notice bias or misinformation, it is essential to point it out. We can do this by writing letters to the editor, participating in public forums, or engaging with media organizations on social media. By actively questioning the media, we contribute to a healthier democracy. For instance, if a news outlet consistently favors one political party, it is our right to express our concerns and ask for more balanced coverage.

Asking for Fair Reporting

As voters, we have the responsibility to ask the media to be fair and provide us with the facts. It is important not to rely solely on one news source. Instead, we should seek information from different outlets with diverse perspectives. This approach allows us to form our own opinions rather than letting the media shape them for us. When we read or watch the news, we should evaluate the information carefully and consider if it presents a balanced view. If it does not, we can look for alternative sources to get a clearer picture.

Making Our Own Decisions

Being well-informed enables us as voters to make our own decisions. We should not let the media dictate how we feel about issues or candidates. A good way to foster independent thinking is to explore various viewpoints. For example, with the important presidential election weeks away, continue researching the candidates' policies from multiple sources. Look for interviews, opinion articles, and fact-checking websites. This process will help in understanding the candidates' positions better.

Understanding the Impact of Media Influence

The influence of media on public opinion cannot be understated. Sometimes, news reports can sway how we perceive events or figures. This can happen through the way headlines are written or the images chosen to accompany a story. For example, if a news article covers a protest and only shows images of violence, it may lead viewers to believe that the entire movement is violent, overlooking the peaceful aspects. As consumers of news, it is essential to approach reports with a critical eye.

The Importance of Misinformation Awareness

In today's world, misinformation spreads quickly through traditional news outlets alike. It is crucial to verify information before accepting it as truth. For example, if you read a startling statistic or claim, take a moment to check its source. Cross-reference it with reliable publications or fact-checking organizations. This habit not only protects you from misleading information but also encourages a culture of accuracy and accountability in the media.

Encouraging Critical Thinking

Encouraging critical thinking skills aids democracy. As Americans, we should question what we hear or read and seek to understand the 'why' behind the headlines. When we attend community discussions or forums it can be beneficial. Engaging in conversations with others about current events can foster diverse perspectives and richer discussions. This process encourages a deeper understanding of issues rather than a surface-level reaction.

Becoming Active Participants in Democracy

Ultimately, engaging with the media is about becoming active participants in our democracy. It is not enough to consume information passively; we have a role in shaping the discourse. We can write letters, participate in discussions, and share information responsibly. Don't hesitate to express your opinion on issues that matter to you and encourage others to do the same.

The Role of Education in Media Literacy

Education should play a significant role in how we understand and interact with media. Schools should teach students about media literacy, helping them become informed citizens. By learning how to analyze news sources and recognize bias, students would gain valuable skills for adult life. This foundation prepares future voters to navigate a complex information landscape with confidence.

Engaging with Local Media

Local media should play a critical role in informing the community. Engaging with local newspapers, radio stations, and TV channels should provide insights into what is happening in your area. These outlets should cover stories that larger media organizations may overlook. Americans need to have a richer information ecosystem that reflects our community's needs and interests.

Building Trust in Media

Building trust between the media and the public is essential for a healthy democracy. Building trust between the media and the public is essential for a healthy democracy. Transparency should be how news is gathered and reported to foster trust. Transparency Transparency should be how news is gathered and reported to foster trust.

Media organizations should be open about their sources and processes. Media organizations should be open about their sources and processes.

This gives the audience confidence in the reliability of the information presented.

When the media adopts a biased stance, it influences the perceptions of average viewers and listeners who depend exclusively on news for their information. It gives the perception that the media is playing in our faces.

Recent complaints have been raised against the media for exhibiting partial views that favor one side while failing to provide the audiences with the necessary facts to form their own opinions. Reports indicate that all prominent prime-time news outlets, along with numerous cable news networks, have colluded in misleading their audiences. This type of behavior poses a significant threat to the democracy that America seeks to uphold.

The Media Has Gone Rogue

The media plays a crucial role in society. Its job is to inform us about current events, share different perspectives, and help shape public opinion. However, there have been times when the media seems to act independently, sometimes straying away from its primary duty of reporting. This behavior has led to a loss of trust between the public and the media, which is concerning because trust is vital for a functioning democracy.

Bias in Reporting

Another aspect of the media going rogue is the apparent bias in reporting. Many outlets have been criticized for favoring one political view over another. This bias can manipulate public perception. For instance, a news channel might report on a political event by emphasizing the negative aspects of one party while downplaying negative outcomes for another party. Audience members may not realize they are consuming a skewed version of events, which reinforces divisions in society.

The Fragmentation of Media

The media landscape is more fragmented than ever before. With numerous outlets available, people often choose sources that align with their existing beliefs. This phenomenon is known as confirmation bias. When individuals surround themselves with similar viewpoints, it can lead to polarization. For instance, debates on social issues become more heated when participants are only exposed to information that supports their views. This fragmentation hinders meaningful dialogue and understanding among different groups. The media has a responsibility to keep issues from becoming divisive.

The Responsibility of the Audience

The media has its failings. However, It is crucial for Americans to critically evaluate their sources of information. Taking the time to verify facts, explore multiple perspectives, and seek out reputable outlets will help improve the overall quality of public discourse. For example, when reading about a complex issue, rather than relying solely on one source, Americans can consult diverse reputable news outlets, academic papers, and expert opinions. Americans can no longer rely on one news media outlet to give us the facts.

Educating the Public

In light of these challenges, educating the public about media literacy is essential. By teaching individuals how to recognize credible sources, identify bias, and analyze the information critically, society can combat misinformation. Schools and communities should hold workshops that focus on these skills. The goal should be to empower citizens to engage thoughtfully with their media consumption.

The Future of the Media

The future of media is uncertain. As Americans begin to see the bias in media outlets, they are turning away from traditional news, and getting their news information from podcasters because they find them to be more authentic. Media outlets need to prioritize integrity, transparency, and quality reporting that may attract audiences who value trustworthy information. This will help them rebuild relationships with their communities, these outlets can regain public confidence. There is also an opportunity for collaborative journalism, where outlets work together to provide thorough, well-researched stories.

The Role of Technology

Advancements in technology can play a significant role in shaping the future of media. Emerging tools, such as artificial intelligence, can assist journalists in fact-checking and identifying false information. While technology can sometimes contribute to the problems, it can also help improve transparency and accountability. Blockchain technology can offer a secure way to track the sources of information, providing clarity on where news comes from and how it was developed.

Holding Media accountable

Accountability is another vital element in restoring trust in the media. Journalistic ethics and standards must be upheld. Independent organizations should monitor media outlets, ensuring they adhere to guidelines of fairness and transparency. Audiences should also feel empowered to demand change. By voicing concerns and holding the media accountable, the public can influence practices within the industry.

The dynamics between the media and the public are evolving. As the landscape changes, both journalists and consumers must adapt to new realities. It is essential to strive for a media environment that fosters trust, promotes understanding, and encourages dialogue among diverse groups. The challenge lies in navigating these changes thoughtfully in a world where information is abundant, but quality varies significantly. Balancing the need for speed with a commitment to truth will be fundamental in shaping the future of the media.

Media organizations should have editorial standards and ethical guidelines that define their commitment to impartial reporting. These guidelines should include principles such as accuracy, fairness, and accountability. For example, major news outlets like the Associated Press or Reuters should have strict protocols for verifying information before publishing it. When these standards are upheld, it helps to maintain public trust.

How Media Watchdogs Keep the Media From Going Rogue

Media watchdogs should play a critical role in maintaining the integrity of journalism. They should serve as an accountability mechanism for news organizations, ensuring that they adhere to ethical standards and provide accurate information. In America, the media is a cornerstone of democracy. In America, the media is the cornerstone of democracy. Therefore, it should inform the public, shape opinions, and hold power accountable. Without effective oversight, media outlets can spread misinformation, favor sensationalism over facts, and undermine public trust. so, media watchdogs should help to keep the media in check.

Media watchdogs should function by monitoring the content produced by news outlets. Analyze newspapers, television broadcasts, and online articles to identify instances of bias, misinformation, or ethical violations. For example, if a news program regularly presents news with a particular political bias, watchdogs should publish a report highlighting this trend. These reports would not only inform the public but also put pressure on media organizations to address their content biases.

Another critical aspect of monitoring should involve evaluating the practices of media organizations. This includes reviewing how stories are sourced and whether they include diverse viewpoints. Media watchdogs conduct audits or surveys to assess how well news organizations reflect the diversity of the communities they serve. If a watchdog finds that certain demographics are consistently underrepresented, they should call on the media to improve its coverage.

Media watchdogs should be responsible for providing training and resources to journalists. They should offer workshops, seminars, and online resources that focus on best practices in journalism. This training should cover topics like ethical reporting, handling sources, and understanding community dynamics. Since watchdogs invest in the education of journalists, this should help improve the quality of news reporting. They should continue to equip journalists with the tools needed to navigate complicated issues and provide facts to stories that resonate with the public.

Holding Media Accountable

Finally, media watchdogs should hold media organizations accountable when they fail to meet established standards. When complaints about unethical practices arise, watchdogs should investigate and issue public statements. This accountability serves as a warning to media outlets that they are being watched and encourages them to reflect on their practices. If a news outlet is found guilty of spreading misinformation, a watchdog should call for corrective action, such as issuing retractions or corrections. This prompt response would maintain credibility in journalism.

Media watchdogs should make sure the media remains accountable and ethical. Through monitoring content and practices, fact-checking claims, providing training, advocating for transparency, engaging with the audience, collaborating with journalists, producing informative reports, and holding media accountable, When they do this they create a stronger foundation for journalism. These efforts would contribute greatly to a well-informed public and a healthier media environment. The role of media watchdogs in modern society needs to be on the side of the American people and help the people make sure that the media upholds the principles of accurate and responsible journalism.

Advertising Influence on Media

Advertising plays a significant role in shaping media content. Media outlets, whether they are newspapers, magazines, television stations, or online platforms, rely on advertising revenue to stay afloat. This dependence on advertising has influenced the type of content that is produced. For example, if a particular product or service is being heavily advertised, media organizations create more content that aligns with the interests of the advertisers. This leads to a situation where the news presented is biased towards advertisers' themes, reducing diversity in the topics covered.

Partisan Views in Media

Partisanship in media has intertwined with advertising. Many media organizations have political affiliations or biases that are reflected in their reporting. This partisanship shapes not only how news is reported but also what news is reported. For instance, a news outlet that aligns itself with a particular political party is focused on issues that the party supports and offers less coverage of opposing viewpoints.

Partisan News Stations

Partisan news refers to reporting that heavily favors one political party over others. In the case of CBS, NBC, ABC, MSNBC, and CNN, American Citizens are seeing that their coverage skews towards the Democratic Party and they don't like it. Americans are witnessing this from the selection of stories, the guests invited for commentary, and the framing of news events. For instance, These networks consistently highlight negative stories about Republican politicians while downplaying similar issues with Democratic officials, and Americans see a pattern of bias.

The Impact of Money on Media Integrity

The media landscape has evolved dramatically over the years, primarily driven by financial interests. When there is too much money involved, it can lead to situations where media outlets prioritize profit over truth. With more financial backing, some organizations may twist stories to attract more viewers or readers. This shift can skew the information being presented to the public. Which is why we need regulations.

Policy Reforms and Regulations

Implementing policy reforms can also help to limit the influence of special interest groups. Governments can create regulations that establish stricter campaign finance laws to reduce the amount of money that special interest groups can contribute to political campaigns. By doing so, the playing field can be leveled, and candidates who prioritize their constituents over financial backers can have a fair chance in elections.

Financial Pressure on Journalism

The quest for revenue affects how news is reported. Advertisers play a crucial role in shaping content. For example, if an advertisement comes from a large corporation, a news outlet may hesitate to publish a story that has negative implications for that company. This financial pressure could result in softened reports or complete omissions of certain facts.

Sensationalism in Reporting

Another consequence of excessive money in the media is sensationalism. To capture the audience's attention, some outlets resort to exaggeration. Instead of focusing on the facts, they may highlight dramatic elements of a story. We know all too well Black Americans in the media for far too long have been sensationalized where the media's portrayal is typically depicted as nothing more than stereotypical. For instance, if a crime occurs, the media might emphasize the violence and danger instead of exploring the root causes such as social issues or economic factors.

"We the People"

When individuals watch the news, they desire fair and accurate reporting. When news outlets disseminate misinformation, it breeds anger and division in communities that they are not part of, allowing them to avoid the repercussions. They remain shielded from the anger and discord. This country is divided between the wealthy and the impoverished, and our democracy hangs by a thread. We have witnessed what a nation devoid of democracy resembles: chaos and destruction.

The power to conduct free and fair elections is what empowers Americans with a voice. It enables Americans to choose the candidate based on facts who is best suited to lead or govern the country.

Without democracy, we, the people, have no control over the trajectory of this great nation. As Americans, we have allowed divisive issues to tear us apart for far too long, to the point where we now feel forced to vote in secrecy. We cannot even discuss our voting preferences for fear of potential harm. This isn't what democracy was meant to embody. We should be able to agree to disagree regarding the outcome. The result of a presidential election, regardless of personal voting choices, should not prevent the newly elected president from serving as president for all.

The influence of money in politics has grown so overwhelming that one can observe the in-fighting among donors, special interest groups, lobbyists, and media journalists. Their anger has overflowed into the media, resulting in Americans growing angry and divisive toward one another. I don't know about you, but I refuse to let provocateurs bait me into a confrontation..." ***You want me to believe... that Omar was a stoolie.... because Sosa said so?"***

I have expressed it before, and I will say it again: Black and White people, have more in common than what divides us. We are losing control of our country because we cannot unite. If we are unable to come together for our own sake, let us do it for the sake of our nation.

Chapter 11

The Great Migration

Black American Men Socio-Economic Timeline in the U.S.

The socio-economic journey of Black American men in the United States has been complex and has seen many significant changes over the years. To understand this timeline, we can look at key periods and events that have shaped their economic status and social standing. From the early days of slavery to modern times, the experiences of Black American men have been influenced by systemic barriers, social movements, and changing laws.

Slavery and Its Legacy

The timeline begins with slavery, which lasted for centuries, and during this time, Black American men were stripped of their rights and forced into labor without compensation. They worked on plantations and in households, with no freedom and little hope for better circumstances. This created a legacy of economic disadvantage. After the Civil War, the Emancipation Proclamation in 1863 and the Thirteenth Amendment in 1865 legally freed enslaved people, but the damage had already been done. Although they were no longer slaves, Black men faced Jim Crow laws, which enforced racial segregation. These laws limited their access to quality education and job opportunities, contributing to generational poverty.

Reconstruction Era

During the Reconstruction era (1865-1877), there were some advances for Black men. They could vote and hold office, and many became part of the political landscape. This period saw the establishment of schools and institutions aimed at educating Black citizens. However, this progress was met with fierce resistance, and shortly after, many of the legal protections were rolled back. The Compromise of 1877 ended Reconstruction and saw the rise of discriminatory practices that oppressed Black men socially and economically.

The Great Migration, which took place from the 1910s to the 1970s, marked another crucial change. Many Black Americans moved from the rural South to urban areas in the North and West in search of better job opportunities. For example, cities like Chicago and Detroit welcomed an influx of Black workers. This migration allowed many Black men to find work in factories and industries, contributing to a growing middle class. However, they also faced challenges such as racial discrimination in employment and housing, limiting their ability to fully benefit from their economic progress.

The Civil Rights Movement

The Civil Rights Movement of the 1950s and 1960s was a pivotal time for Black American men. Activists fought against segregation and for equal rights, leading to landmark legislation like the Civil Rights Act of 1964 and the Voting Rights Act of 1965. These laws made it unlawful to discriminate based on race, aiming to level the playing field. Black men began to make strides in various professions, including politics, education, and business. For example, figures like John Lewis and Jesse Jackson emerged as prominent leaders advocating for change. Despite this progress, systemic racism and socioeconomic disparities remained, affecting their overall success.

Economic Challenges in the Late 20th Century

The late 20th century continued to present economic challenges. The manufacturing jobs that had once provided stable incomes began to decline due to globalization and changes in industry. Many Black men lost their jobs and faced high unemployment rates. The crack cocaine epidemic in the 1980s further exacerbated issues within Black communities, leading to significant rates of incarceration among young Black men. This not only impacted families but also limited economic opportunities for those released from prison, creating a cycle of poverty.

Education and Social Mobility

Education plays a critical role in the socioeconomic status of Black men today. Despite historical barriers, progress has been made, with more Black men enrolling in colleges and universities than ever before. Initiatives such as mentoring programs and scholarship opportunities are essential in supporting their educational endeavors. However, challenges remain, including student loan debt and underfunded schools in predominantly Black neighborhoods. Access to quality education is vital for breaking the cycles of poverty and ensuring that Black men can attain upward social mobility.

Current Socio-Economic Landscape

Today, the socio-economic landscape for Black American men reflects a mix of progress and ongoing challenges. Despite advancements, disparities still exist in income, employment, and home ownership compared to their white counterparts. Efforts to address systemic inequalities continue, and discussions around reparations for descendants of enslaved people and initiatives aimed at closing the racial wealth gap are more prominent. Activism and advocacy remain essential components in this ongoing fight for equality and equitable economic opportunities.

It's crucial to continue addressing the socio-economic inequities facing Black American men. Initiatives aimed at creating pathways to good jobs, affordable housing, and quality education are essential. Supporting Black-owned businesses and advocating for fair legislation will also play critical roles in building a more equitable future. With these efforts, the socio-economic trajectory of Black American men can change for the better, promoting not just individual prosperity but the prosperity of entire communities.

The timeline of Black American men's socio-economic status in the U.S. reflects not only their struggles but also their resilience. Each phase of this journey has shaped the current reality and continues to influence future generations. Understanding this history is vital in working towards genuine equality and justice in society.

Mental Health and PTSD in Black Male Slaves

Understanding mental health is key to grasping the experiences of Black male slaves in history. Their lives were filled with trauma, pain, and ongoing stress from being enslaved. Slavery exposed Black male slaves to severe physical and emotional abuse. They lived in constant fear of violence, were often separated from their families, and had little control over their lives.

The capture and transport to plantations were also traumatic. Many men experienced violent disruptions in their lives, leaving behind their families and homes. This separation caused feelings of grief and loss, as some men would never see their loved ones again, leading to deep emotional pain. Over time, these stressors could significantly affect a person's mental health and contribute to PTSD.

Societal views at that time also impacted the mental health of Black men. They were often treated as property instead of people, which could strip away their sense of identity and self-worth. This harsh environment could worsen their trauma and lead to feelings of isolation.

During this historical period, treatment for mental health problems was almost nonexistent. The conditions were also not supportive of healing. Even after emancipation, the psychological wounds from slavery didn't disappear. The impact of trauma continues to affect the descendants of enslaved individuals. Many Black men today may struggle with PTSD or other mental health issues related to ongoing discrimination and social challenges. **The history of trauma faced by their ancestors influences their present mental health.**

Understanding Psychological Trauma in Black American Males

Psychological trauma can deeply affect individuals, impacting their emotional and mental well-being. For Black American males today, this trauma is often linked to the historical context of slavery. Slavery was not just a physical experience; it left psychological scars that can persist through generations. The legacy of slavery created an environment filled with pain and suffering, which still influences the lives of many Black American males.

Historical Context of Slavery

Slavery in America lasted for centuries, during which countless Black individuals were subjected to inhumane treatment. The trauma caused by the brutal experiences of forced labor, family separations, and violence is significant. Many Black families lost their loved ones, faced constant fear, and lived in a society that considered them less than human. This historical trauma did not end with the abolition of slavery; instead, it contributed to ongoing cycles of disadvantage and mental health challenges.

Intergenerational Trauma

The effects of slavery do not just affect those who lived through it but continue to impact their descendants. This phenomenon is known as intergenerational trauma. For instance, a Black male today may struggle with feelings of inadequacy or fear, stemming from the collective pain experienced by his ancestors. These feelings may manifest in various ways, such as anxiety, depression, or issues with self-esteem.

Understanding this concept is crucial for recognizing how historical events shape present-day realities.

Societal Impacts

In addition to personal trauma, societal structures have also played a role in perpetuating the effects of slavery. Systemic racism and discrimination have remained prevalent throughout American history, continuing to create barriers for Black American males. These barriers often include limited access to quality education, employment opportunities, and healthcare. Such inequalities can lead to a sense of hopelessness and disconnection from society.

Importance of Community Support

Community plays a significant role in the healing process. Supportive relationships with family, friends, and trusted individuals can help Black American males feel understood and validated. Engaging in community activities can foster connection and reduce feelings of isolation. For example, joining local organizations that focus on mental health and wellness can create a network of support. Shared experiences often provide a sense of belonging and reassurance that helps individuals cope with their trauma.

Understanding the Impact of Systemic Racism

It is essential to acknowledge that the effects of psychological trauma in Black American males are often intertwined with systemic racism. Institutions that perpetuate inequality can exacerbate feelings of helplessness and anxiety. Understanding this connection allows for more targeted efforts to support healing and growth. Addressing systemic issues can create a more supportive environment for Black individuals, which is essential for recovery.

Trauma is a serious emotional response to a disturbing event or series of events. It can make someone feel scared, anxious, or overwhelmed. Trauma can happen after events like accidents, violence, abuse, or natural disasters. People who experience trauma may have trouble sleeping, focusing, or feeling safe.

Intergenerational Trauma and its Effects on Black American Males Today

Intergenerational trauma refers to the transmission of the effects of trauma from one generation to the next. For Black American males, this trauma can be traced back to a long history of systemic oppression, slavery, and ongoing discrimination. The historical experiences of Black Americans have created a complex set of challenges that affect their mental, emotional, and physical well-being today. This can manifest in various ways, affecting how they relate to themselves and others. Understanding this trauma is important to addressing the needs of Black American males in modern society.

To grasp the impact of intergenerational trauma, it is vital to recognize how earlier experiences shape current realities. For example, the legacy of slavery has instilled a sense of distrust in institutions, including healthcare, education, and law enforcement among Black American males. This distrust can lead to reluctance to seek help for mental health issues or participating in programs designed to foster personal growth. The trauma also affects family structures, where the absence of stable male role models may perpetuate cycles of dysfunction, creating environments that struggle with emotional expression and support.

Societal perceptions can also play a significant role in how Black American males view themselves and their place in the world. Media representations often reflect negative stereotypes that reinforce feelings of inadequacy or aggression. Many Black males grow up internalizing these views, leading to low self-esteem and a sense of hopelessness. These feelings can trigger a range of maladaptive behaviors. For instance, some may engage in substance abuse as a coping mechanism while others might express their pain through violence. It becomes crucial to challenge and change these narratives to promote healthier self-identities

.

Moreover, the community environment plays a significant role in how trauma manifests. Neighborhoods with high violence rates often create a prevailing culture of survival. Here, young Black males may feel the need to adopt tough personas to navigate potential threats. This reaction is a learned behavior stemming from trauma, which teaches them that vulnerability can be dangerous. As such, emotional shutdown becomes a common strategy for coping with everyday life. Community initiatives aimed at creating safe spaces for emotional sharing are essential in breaking these cycles. Programs for mentorship and building trust can provide these individuals with alternate models of masculinity that are based on strength through vulnerability.

Education is another key area where intergenerational trauma affects Black American males. Structural inequalities in education systems often lead to lower performance outcomes. For example, schools in predominantly Black neighborhoods often lack adequate resources, experienced teachers, and extracurricular opportunities. This educational disadvantage can contribute to a sense of disenfranchisement, which perpetuates the cycle of trauma. Research indicates that when Black males are provided with mentors and role models who understand their unique challenges, they are more likely to succeed academically. It is important to invest in educational systems that recognize and address these disparities.

Employment opportunities also intersect with intergenerational trauma. Black American males often face barriers to employment due to systemic racism, criminal records, or a lack of networking opportunities. These barriers not only affect their economic stability but also their mental health and self-worth. Many feel stuck in low-paying jobs with no clear path for advancement. Initiatives that provide job training, resume building, and interview practice can empower Black males to pursue better job prospects. This empowerment fosters a sense of agency that counteracts feelings of helplessness associated with trauma.

Mental health is a crucial aspect often overlooked in discussions about intergenerational trauma. Many Black American males may feel stigmatized when seeking help for mental health issues. They may have been socialized to believe that seeking help represents weakness. However, mental health is vital for overall well-being. Culturally competent mental health services tailored to meet the needs of Black males are necessary. These services should provide safe, understanding environments where they can express their feelings without judgment. Community programs that prioritize mental health education can aid in breaking down these barriers.

Family dynamics also play a significant role in the effects of intergenerational trauma. The absence of fathers or male figures can lead to unresolved emotional issues in Black males. Programs that promote fatherhood involvement or provide support for single mothers can create more nurturing family environments. When these males receive proper support at home, they are more likely to develop healthy relationships and break the cycle of trauma. Family therapy can also help address historical grievances and improve communication among family members.

Acknowledge the role of cultural heritage and identity in healing intergenerational trauma. Celebrating culture and instilling pride in heritage can empower Black American males to embrace their identity. Activities that promote cultural education, such as art, music, and storytelling, can facilitate discussion about past experiences and their impact on current mental health. This process can encourage healing and connection to one's roots and ancestors, which can be therapeutic in overcoming trauma.

Building supportive communities is essential for addressing the effects of intergenerational trauma. Safe spaces where Black American males can engage in open dialogue about their experiences are vital. Community organizations should facilitate workshops, focus groups, and social gatherings that promote understanding and healing. These platforms allow individuals to share their stories, recognize common struggles, and develop strategies for coping together. Strengthening community ties can create a network of support that eases the burden of trauma.

In addressing intergenerational trauma among Black American males, collaboration between community members, educators, mental health professionals, and policymakers is key. Together, we can work toward comprehensive solutions that tackle the root causes of trauma. Policies that focus on improving access to quality education, healthcare, and job opportunities can significantly impact the lives of Black males. Advocacy for systemic change at local and national levels is essential to create a more equitable society.

Recognizing the impact of intergenerational trauma is the first step toward healing. It is important to engage in conversations that promote understanding and awareness of these issues. *By fostering an environment where Black American males feel seen and heard, we can begin to dismantle the burdens of trauma.* Through education, community support, and mental health resources, we can contribute to breaking the cycle and paving the way for healthier futures.

Compensation to Black American Males for Intergenerational Trauma

Intergenerational trauma refers to the psychological and emotional effects that trauma can have on future generations. This phenomenon is particularly relevant when discussing the historical and ongoing injustices faced by Black American men. The idea of compensating these individuals for their suffering is rooted in a deep understanding of how trauma can persist and affect people's lives long after the original events have occurred.

Understanding Intergenerational Trauma

To better grasp intergenerational trauma, it is important to define what this concept entails. This type of trauma occurs when the effects of a traumatic event are passed down from one generation to another. For example, children of those who experienced slavery, segregation, or systemic racism may carry emotional and psychological scars that manifest in various ways. This can include issues such as anxiety, depression, and feelings of low self-worth. Understanding this can shed light on why recognizing and compensating for this trauma is crucial.

The historical context of Black American males is filled with hardships and suffering. From slavery to Jim Crow laws and modern-day systemic racism, these experiences have created layers of trauma. For instance, the legacy of slavery has not only affected the immediate descendants of enslaved individuals but has cast a shadow over entire communities. Policies such as redlining and unequal funding for schools have perpetuated economic and social disparities. This ongoing cycle of disadvantage impacts the mental health of individuals and collects over generations.

The Impact of Trauma

The impact of trauma on Black American males is evident in various areas of life. Mental health issues can arise, making individuals more likely to struggle in their personal and professional lives. For example, a young Black male may face discrimination in the workplace, leading to stress and anxiety. This stress can be compounded by the expectations and experiences passed down from previous generations, creating a heavy burden. By acknowledging this impact, we can understand why reparations or compensation might be necessary to help alleviate some of these burdens.

Ultimately, promoting resilience and healing among Black American males requires collective efforts from individuals, communities, and institutions. By working together and acknowledging the multifaceted issue of intergenerational trauma, we can create a more supportive society. This society recognizes the importance of compensation and actively promotes healing, education, and understanding for future generations. Each small step forward contributes to the journey toward healing and restoration for those affected.

The Need for Slavery Among Democratic Party

In the early years of American history, the issue of slavery sparked a significant division among political parties. The Democratic Party's roots can be traced back to the early 19th century, and during this time, many of its members openly supported the institution of slavery. Democrats, particularly those from the Southern states, believed that slavery was essential for their agrarian economy. They argued that enslaved labor was the foundation of their prosperity. Large plantations relied heavily on the work of enslaved people to cultivate crops like cotton and tobacco.

Democrats saw slavery as a necessary practice to maintain their way of life. They believed that without slavery, their economic stability would be threatened. This belief was fortified by social and cultural norms that dehumanized African Americans, painting them as inferior. The support for slavery among Democrats was not just a political stance but a deeply ingrained societal attitude. They fought against any legislative changes that might threaten the institution of slavery, fearing that emancipation would lead to chaos and a collapse of their economic system.

Neurological Complications

To comprehend the full impact of slavery, it's essential to look back at the conditions in which enslaved people lived. Enslaved black Americans were subjected to brutal treatment, including physical violence, emotional abuse, and severe restrictions on their freedoms. This intense stress and trauma during critical periods of development can lead to changes in brain development. Studies have shown that extreme stress can affect how the brain grows, particularly in areas related to stress response, emotion regulation, and executive function.

The Rise of the Republican Party

In response to the growing divisions over slavery, the Republican Party emerged in the 1850s. This party was founded on the principles of opposing the expansion of slavery into western territories. Many Republicans believed that slavery was morally wrong and incompatible with the ideals of freedom and democracy. Prominent figures like Abraham Lincoln advocated for the rights of African Americans and sought to limit the reach of slavery. The party attracted a diverse group of supporters who were united by this common goal.

Republicans viewed the fight against slavery as both a moral obligation and a political necessity. They argued that the expansion of slavery would not only harm African Americans but also threaten white laborers. They believed that the presence of slavery in the territories would create unfair competition for jobs. This ideology resonated with many, leading to increased support for Republican candidates. The party's platform clearly stated its opposition to the extension of slavery, which set the stage for a significant political showdown.

The Role of Abraham Lincoln

Abraham Lincoln played a crucial role in the Republican Party's efforts to end slavery. As the party's presidential candidate in 1860, Lincoln's election signaled a turning point in American history. His stance against the expansion of slavery angered many Southern Democrats, ultimately leading to their secession and the Civil War. Lincoln's leadership was marked by his commitment to preserving the Union, but he also understood that slavery was a central issue that needed to be addressed.

Lincoln's Emancipation Proclamation in 1863 was a pivotal moment. This executive order declared that all enslaved people in Confederate-held territory were to be set free. While it did not end slavery entirely, it shifted the war's focus and made the abolition of slavery a primary goal for the Union. Lincoln's decision illustrated his belief that ending slavery was essential for the nation's moral and political future. It also galvanized support for the Union cause, inspiring many to join the fight.

The Abolition of Slavery

The conflict between Democrats and Republicans culminated in the passage of the Thirteenth Amendment in 1865. This amendment formally abolished slavery in the United States, marking a significant victory for the Republican Party and its allies. The struggles of the Civil War had underscored the necessity of ending slavery, and this constitutional change reflected the shifting attitudes toward human rights. What had started as a political disagreement evolved into a moral imperative that found support across various sectors of society.

The Thirteenth Amendment was not merely a declaration; it required a transformation in how American society viewed race and equality. It laid the groundwork for future civil rights advancements. However, the end of slavery did not mean that racial discrimination and inequality ended immediately. The legacy of slavery left deep scars in the fabric of American society, which would result in ongoing struggles for civil rights.

The Republican Party and the 14th Amendment

The Republican Party played a crucial role in the implementation of the 14th Amendment, which was ratified in 1868. This amendment was important for the protection of the rights of Black Americans following the Civil War. It aimed to guarantee citizenship to anyone born in the United States, which included formerly enslaved individuals. This was a significant change in the law, as it directly challenged the previous system that allowed for the enslavement of people based on their race.

The 14th Amendment established that all citizens, regardless of race, were entitled to equal protection under the law. This meant that state laws could not discriminate against anyone based on their skin color. For example, if a state passed a law that restricted the rights of Black citizens, that law could be challenged in court based on the 14th Amendment. This was a powerful tool for protecting the rights of individuals and ensuring that the government could not unfairly target a group of people.

However, implementing the 14th Amendment was not an easy task. Many Southern states resisted these changes, as they were still holding onto their old ways of life that depended heavily on the oppression of Black Americans. The Republican Party worked hard to enforce the amendment and ensure that it was upheld. They sent federal troops to the South to protect Black citizens and to help enforce the new laws that came from the amendment. This was necessary to create a safer environment for Black Americans to exercise their rights.

The 15th Amendment and Voting Rights

The Republican Party also advocated for the 15th Amendment, which was ratified in 1870. This amendment aimed to protect the voting rights of Black men. The 15th Amendment states that the right to vote cannot be denied based on race, color, or previous condition of servitude. This was a monumental step toward achieving equality, as it granted Black Americans the ability to participate in the democratic process.

To illustrate the importance of the 15th Amendment, consider the situation prior to its ratification. Before the amendment, many Southern states employed various tactics to disenfranchise Black voters. These included literacy tests, poll taxes, and other forms of intimidation at the polls. The 15th Amendment aimed to put an end to these practices and ensure that all citizens had a fair chance to vote.

In the years following the ratification of the 15th Amendment, many Black men successfully registered to vote and participated in elections. For example, during the Reconstruction era, several Black men were elected to public office. This was a significant step toward increased representation for Black Americans in government. However, the journey did not end there, as many states continued to find loopholes and ways to suppress Black voter turnout.

The Implementation of Jim Crow Laws by the Democratic Party

The Democratic Party played a significant role in the introduction and implementation of Jim Crow laws in the United States. These laws were a series of state and local statutes that enforced racial segregation in the Southern United States. Following the end of the Reconstruction era in the late 19th century, many Southern states sought to maintain white supremacy and control over the African American population. The Democratic Party, which was dominant in the South during this time, supported these laws to ensure that African Americans remained marginalized.

After the Civil War, the Reconstruction period aimed to integrate newly freed slaves into American society. However, this era faced intense backlash from many white Southerners who were unhappy with the changes. The Democratic Party, composed largely of Southern whites, opposed the policies of Reconstruction. As federal troops withdrew from the South in 1877, the Democratic Party regained control and quickly began to roll back the advancements made by African Americans. This shift led to the introduction of laws that would shape the South for decades.

Definition and Purpose of Jim Crow Laws 1960'S

Jim Crow laws are defined as state and local laws that enforced racial segregation. The term "Jim Crow" originally referred to a black character in a minstrel show. Over time, it became synonymous with the system of oppression targeted towards African Americans. The laws aimed to establish a separate but equal status for African Americans, often resulting in the systematic disenfranchisement and social, economic, and political disadvantage of black individuals. The purpose of these laws was clear: to maintain white dominance in all areas of life including education, transportation, and public facilities.

Segregation in Public Facilities

One of the most visible outcomes of Jim Crow laws was the segregation of public facilities. Schools, restaurants, parks, and even water fountains were designated for whites only or blacks only. For example, there were separate schools for white and black children, with schools for African Americans often receiving far less funding and resources. The educational disparity was significant and led to a long-term impact on African American students' opportunities and outcomes. The Democratic Party's support for these laws made it difficult for African Americans to break the cycle of poverty and lack of education.

Voting Restrictions

Another critical aspect of Jim Crow laws was voter suppression aimed at African Americans. The Democratic Party implemented measures like literacy tests, poll taxes, and understanding clauses to ensure that African Americans faced barriers when trying to vote. These measures were often arbitrary and unfairly applied, disenfranchising a vast majority of black voters. For instance, a white voter might be given an easier literacy test than a black voter, effectively disenfranchising African Americans even though they had the legal right to vote.

Economic Disadvantages

Jim Crow laws also entrenched economic disparities between white and black populations. The laws restricted African Americans' ability to own businesses or own property in certain areas. They were often relegated to low-paying jobs with little opportunity for advancement. For example, many African Americans worked as sharecroppers, a system that kept them in perpetual debt to white landowners. The Democratic Party's policies and support of these laws solidified a system that limited economic mobility for African Americans.

Resistance to Jim Crow Laws

Despite the oppressive nature of Jim Crow laws, there was significant resistance from African Americans and their allies. Many individuals stood up against these injustices, organizing protests and advocacy groups. The NAACP (National Association for the Advancement of Colored People) was founded in 1909 and played a pivotal role in fighting against segregation and discriminatory laws. Their efforts brought national attention to the struggles faced by African Americans and highlighted the detrimental effects of Jim Crow laws.

Legacy of Jim Crow Laws

The legacy of Jim Crow laws is still felt in contemporary society. The systemic inequalities established during this era have lasting effects on education, employment, and housing for African Americans. Persistent racial disparities in wealth, health care, and access to opportunities can often be traced back to the injustices of the Jim Crow era. Understanding the role of the Democratic Party in implementing these laws is essential to addressing the ongoing impacts of racial discrimination.

The implementation of Jim Crow laws by the Democratic Party was a critical juncture in American history that shaped the social landscape of the nation. From enforcing racial segregation to suppressing black votes, these laws aimed to maintain power and control over African Americans. The resistance to these laws and the eventual changes brought about by the civil rights movement illustrates the ongoing struggle for equality and justice in the face of institutional oppression.

Chapter 12

Exodus to Empowerment

My journey has led me to a profound understanding and reflection. This is one of the reasons I chose to discuss the history of Black Americans in the United States, as well as to delineate the distinctions between the two parties as I see them. American history has often been a narrative clouded by misinformation, making it exceedingly difficult to uncover the truth. I hope that this book serves as a vital historical resource to remind us of the importance of truth-telling and preserving history, enabling us to heal from past wounds and ensuring that our children grasp its lessons. By acknowledging rather than denying our historical legacy, we can gain insights that will facilitate healing and collective progress. More importantly, this awareness will ensure that we never repeat the mistakes of the past.

I have witnessed the enduring effects of past traumas on Black American men, including fathers, grandfathers, brothers, uncles, nephews, cousins, and friends. These men frequently attempt to suppress their trauma, perhaps hoping that it will merely dissipate over time. As a Black American woman, I can empathize with the anguish that resonates among them. I comprehend the challenges that arise from these experiences. Many people find it hard to deal with this pain. The subject feels too burdensome and too delicate, and numerous individuals find it challenging to even initiate the conversation.

Society has many opinions on this matter. A common refrain is that slavery is in the past and that we should just move on. This view ignores a key aspect of our history: Jim Crow laws, which were in effect as recently as the 1960s and 1970s. Many of you may have parents or grandparents who lived through that brutal struggle for civil rights. While slavery is something we would like to forget, the intergenerational trauma stemming from it remains prevalent today. This trauma affects our everyday lives in ways that can be hard to pinpoint, including neurological implications, which can create barriers to mental health and overall well-being.

It's important to clarify that Black Americans are not victims in the traditional sense. Black American Males feel that they have been victimized by a political system that refuses to take full responsibility for the harm and oppression they've inflicted. And what they are saying is that this political group continues to perpetuate injustices even today. Black American men have voted for the Democratic Party for decades.

If you look closely at many Democratic-run states, you can see the urgent need for repair in Black neighborhoods. These areas are often left broken and underserved. There's a notable lack of quality education and educational resources, including access to libraries and health clinics. Many of these neighborhoods are starved for job opportunities, which further compounds the struggles faced by residents. The amenities that many others take for granted are often out of reach for these communities, leading to cycles of poverty and despair.

Black American men have come to realize that the Democratic Party is responsible for the oppression of Black Americans. The Democratic Party has put enmity between them and their women. Historically, it was the Democratic Party that didn't want slavery to end, they resisted granting Black men the right to vote and fought against Black citizenship. They also opposed equal protection for Black people, and they were instrumental in the formation of the Ku Klux Klan, and allied with the Confederacy.

It was the Democratic Party that implemented the Jim Crow Laws, which have stunted economic growth to this day and have leveraged their influence in corporations, entities, and establishments to prevent the economic advancement of Black Americans. The policies they have enacted have restricted access to essential services that would promote growth and development.

They dangle reparations like a carrot. The blatant intimidation and bullying from this party are relentless. In the eighties, they imported Black immigrants to replace Black American men and women; now they're bringing in migrants to replace our children and their generation. Yet, as a society, we passively observe.

Meanwhile, each generation continues to confront the same daunting obstacles, perpetuating a cycle of inequality and hardship. Moreover, this immigration issue is not only impacting the Black community but also low- to middle-class White Americans.

For sixty years, Black American men have steadfastly voted for the Democratic Party, yearning for transformative change. They have patiently awaited the party to acknowledge and address their concerns, yet that recognition has consistently evaded them. Black American men have faced numerous challenges throughout history, and this struggle continues today. They work hard every day to provide for their families, often juggling multiple jobs to make ends meet.

Despite their efforts, many find their economic status stagnant, leaving them frustrated and disheartened. This reality reflects a broader issue where their contributions go unnoticed, leaving them feeling like invisible members of society. For instance, many Black men take on jobs in industries like construction, transportation, Maintenance, sanitation, security, warehouse, Drivers, etc. where they often face long hours and demanding physical labor. Yet, when payday arrives, the paychecks rarely reflect the hard work they've put in.

In addition to their work, many Black American men strive to be positive role models for their children. They understand the importance of education and are often deeply involved in their children's schooling. They attend parent-teacher meetings, help with homework, and encourage their kids to strive for excellence. However, despite these efforts, they sometimes feel like their dreams for a better future are beyond their reach. Making them realize that the political party they have supported for so long, hasn't been supportive of them.

The Forgotten Demographic

When discussing government support, many low-middle-class Americans feel that they are the forgotten demographic. The focus often seems directed toward aiding immigrants and wealthier segments of the population. This shift in priorities has left Low and Middle-class Black and White Americans feeling abandoned. They see resources being allocated for programs that benefit new arrivals while their own needs remain unaddressed.

Take for example job opportunities, Companies are prioritizing the hiring of immigrants over local workers, which has created feelings of anger among those who have lived and worked in their communities for years. This can lead to a dangerous division where people feel pitted against one another, rather than standing together to demand equitable treatment from their government.

The injustices inflicted upon Black Americans are layered and complex. Imagine growing up in a community where your school lacks proper funding, and where you face daily challenges simply because of the neighborhood you live in. These experiences do not only affect individuals; they affect families and entire communities. The mental and emotional toll of these circumstances can lead to feelings of despair, making it harder to break the cycle. Every day, the struggles faced by residents in these neighborhoods remind us of the political and social systems that have failed us.

The Role of Corporations and Institutions

It's also essential to recognize how corporations and institutions play a role in this ongoing oppression. The influence of the Democratic Party is evident in countless organizations, where it shapes policies that resonate through different sectors of our lives. These institutions often benefit from the very same communities that they seem to neglect. Advocacy for change requires not just awareness but action from these entities to help uplift communities. It is not enough to simply acknowledge the struggles; meaningful support and investment are necessary for real improvement. It's time to take ownership.

We must confront these painful truths. It takes a collective effort from individuals, communities, political representatives, and organizations to foster change. Steps to uplift neighborhoods include advocating for better educational resources, improved healthcare facilities, and job training programs. It's about creating pathways for young people and ensuring they have access to opportunities that allow them to thrive. It's time to break the chains of generational trauma and build stronger futures for these generations and generations to come.

Black and White Unity

Throughout American history, there have been significant events that contributed to the division between Black and White Americans. From the early days of slavery to the Civil Rights Movement, various social, political, and economic factors have created barriers to unity.

Socioeconomic status has also played a critical role in the division. Media representation plays a significant role in shaping perceptions and reinforcing stereotypes. For many years, the portrayal of Black Americans in the media has been often negative or one-dimensional.

Political leaders exploit racial tensions for their own benefit, leading to polarization. The education system is another crucial factor in understanding this divide. Schools often reflect the communities they serve, and in many cases, they are segregated by race and socioeconomic status.

Allyship is another important aspect of fostering unity. White individuals can play a crucial role by becoming allies with Black Americans. This involves recognizing privilege and using it to advocate for change. Allies can support Black voices and work to dismantle systems of oppression.

It is essential to recognize that unity is a continuous journey. It involves acknowledging the past, understanding the present, and working together to create a better future. Both Black and White Americans must be willing to confront their biases and engage in the challenging conversations necessary for growth.

Finally, Black American men have faced numerous adversities throughout history. These challenges have persisted from the onset of their experiences in America to the present day. When you understand their plight, you grasp the full breadth of their reality. There is a significant misconception surrounding the success of Black American men.

When discussing their achievements, people often point to Black American celebrities as examples to uplift others. It is all too common to hear, "If they can do it, so can you." This statement is profoundly misleading. The truth is that not every Black American man aspires to be a celebrity or an athlete, nor do they have the same opportunities as those who have attained fame. Furthermore, not all scouts are in search of 20 million Black American males who can excel in sports. Consequently, not every individual, whether Black or White, will achieve fame.

Many Black American men pursue professional careers, while others opt for ordinary jobs, diligently working to provide for their families. Some Black American men prefer a quiet life with their wives and children, praising God. They desire to raise their families in safe neighborhoods, with access to quality schools and educational resources within their communities. Not every Black American man seeks fame; therefore, it is erroneous to equate the accomplishments of a few with the potential of many.

These men, who manage their households through day jobs, receive little recognition and are often overlooked. This oversight in politics, having voted for the Democratic Party for over sixty years, has brought them to a crossroads. Black American men have been loyal allies of the Democratic Party while watching other allies receive reforms, community uplifting, and opportunities to start businesses and achieve upward mobility in exchange for their loyal alliance with the Democratic Party.

The support of Black American men for the Democratic Party over the last sixty years went unnoticed.

Black men seek the same aspirations that all men do: the capacity to provide for their families, access to quality education for themselves and their children, lower taxes, opportunities for entrepreneurship, the ability to save and purchase a home, and the chance to nurture their children in a secure environment laden with resources for their flourishing. This pursuit has proven to be an insurmountable challenge for Black men aligned with the Democratic Party. Over the past eight years, we have observed a significant shift as Black men increasingly turn to the Republican Party, and as we approach 2024, this phenomenon is more pertinent than ever. Black American men have reached a breaking point, and we are now witnessing a monumental paradigm shift in the voting landscape, heralding a movement from Exodus to Empowerment.

I Hear a Song coming On

Alone in a room

It's just me and You

I feel so lost

'Cause I don't know what to do

Now what if choose the wrong thing to do

I'm so afraid, afraid of disappointing You

… So I need to talk to You

And ask You for Your guidance

Especially today

When my life is so cloudy

Guide me until I'm sure

I open up my heart, ooh yeah

… My hopes and dreams

Are fading fast

I'm all burned out

And I don't think my strength's gonna last

So I'm crying out

Crying out to You

Lord I know that You're the only one

Who is able to pull me through

… So I need to talk to You

And ask You for Your guidance

Especially today

When my world seems so cloudy, lord

Guide me until I'm sure

I open up my heart, oh yeah, yes I do

… So show me how

To do things Your way

Don't let me make the same mistakes

Over and over again

Your will be done

And I'll be the one

To make sure that it's carried out

And in me, I don't want any doubt

That's why

… I wanna to talk to You, excited

And ask You for Your guidance

Especially today

When my world seems a little bit cloudy

Lord, You can guide me through

That's why I open up, I open up my heart, my heart, my heart

… All I need to do

Is just hear a single word from You, ooh

I open up my heart

Just one word could make

A difference in what I do lord

Guide me until I'm sure

I open, I open, I open, I open my heart

… Whoa, You just say one word, one word, one word, one word, one word

I open up, I open up, open up my heart to you, to you

You're the lover of my soul

The Captain of my sea

I need a word from You

That's why I open up my heart

The End

The Lord is my Sheppard

The Lord is my shepherd; I shall not want.

He maketh me to lie down in green pastures: he leadeth me beside the still waters.

He restoreth my soul: he leadeth me in the paths of righteousness for his name's sake.

Yea, though I walk through the valley of the shadow of death, I will fear no evil:

for thou art with me; thy rod and thy staff they comfort me.

Thou preparest a table before me in the presence of mine enemies:

thou anointest my head with oil; my cup runneth over.

Surely goodness and mercy shall follow me all the days of my life:

and I will dwell in the house of the Lord forever.

Psalm: 23

For God so loved the world

that He gave His only begotten Son,

that whoever believes in Him

should not perish

but have everlasting life.

17

For God did not send His Son

into the world to condemn the world,

but that the world

through Him might be saved.

18

He who believes in Him

is not condemned;

but he who does not believe

is condemned already,

because he has not believed

in the name of the only begotten Son of God.